Poststructuralist theory and classroom practice

Bronwyn Davies

Deakin University

This book has been produced as part of the study materials for ELE716 *Language and Gender*, which is one of the units offered by the Faculty of Education in Deakin University's Open Campus Program. It has been prepared for the unit team, whose members are:
Jill Blackmore
Bronwyn Davies (consultant)
Lesley Farrell
Pam Gilbert (consultant)
Barbara Kamler (chair)
Rod Maclean

The study materials include:
Bronwyn Davies, *Poststructuralist Theory and Classroom Practice**
Pam Gilbert, *Gender Stories and the Language Classroom**
Language and Gender: Study Guide
Language and Gender: Reader

*These books may be purchased from Deakin University Press, Deakin University, Geelong, Victoria, Australia 3217.
More titles may be added to this list from time to time.
Enrolled students also receive a unit guide.

Published by Deakin University, Geelong, Victoria, Australia 3217
Distributed by Deakin University Press
First published 1994

Edited, designed and typeset by Deakin University Publishing Unit
Printed by Deakin University

National Library of Australia
Cataloguing-in-publication data

    Davies, Bronwyn, 1945– .
      Poststructuralist theory and classroom practice.

      Bibliography.
      ISBN 0 7300 1728 1.

      1. Classroom management. 2. Structuralism. 3. Gender identity.
      4. Educational equalisation. I. Deakin University. Faculty of
      Education. Open Campus Program. II. Title

    371. 1024

Acknowledgments

There are a number of people who have contributed to this book in different ways. These include students with whom I have worked on different projects reported here such as the collective biography work on first awareness of gender at the State University of New York at Binghamton; the student in the gender and education course there who gave me permission to use her essay; students in Joseph Schneider's men and film class at Drake University who talked to me about *Pretty Woman*, and students in the feminist theory and research methodology course at the University of New England who worked on the collective biography menstruation workshops—these include Debra Phillips, Sylvia Belsey, Angie Smith, Clare Walsh-Clarke and Norma Koehne. Several of my postgraduate students have also read and commented on all or parts of this book in helpful ways. These include Margaret Bearlin, Jill Golden, Simon Swinson and Norma Koehne. To all of these students I give my thanks.

As well, I am indebted to Chas Banks who worked with the primary school study groups that were set up as part of an ARC project on which she worked with me. Some of the interviews and discussions in those groups are included here. To Chas and to the students in those study groups I also give my thanks.

'Mr Good' and his students, who appear in chapter 2, provided me with a glimpse of their everyday lives in their classroom, allowing me to interact with their world in ways they might not have anticipated. To them I owe my special thanks.

I am particularly indebted to those friends and colleagues who have read and talked to me about this and other of my work. These include Carolyn Baker, Max Lawson, Margaret Somerville and Johanna Wyn. To these people my special thanks. And, of course, I am indebted to Barbara Kamler who asked me to write this book and who gave me invaluable editorial feedback in the final stages.

The quotation on pp. 4–5 is reproduced from Bronwyn Davies, 'The problem of desire', *Social Problems*, vol. 37, no. 4, 1990, p. 507, by permission of the author and publisher; © Society for the Study of Social Problems. Quotations on pp. 6–8, 10–15 & 85–6 are reproduced from Bronwyn Davies, *Shards of Glass: Children Reading and Writing beyond Gendered Identities*, Allen & Unwin, Sydney, 1993, pp. 53–5, 102–7 & 27–9, by permission of the author and publisher. The quotation on pp. 20–1 and figures 1, 2 & 3 on p. 21 are reproduced from Raymond McDermott, Kids make sense: An ethnographic account of the interactional management of success and failure in one first grade classroom, unpublished PhD thesis, Stanford

University, Calif., 1976, pp. 94–5, 43, 47 & 133, by permission of the author. The quotation on pp. 23–5 is reproduced from Bronwyn Davies & Rom Harré, 'Positioning: The discursive production of selves', *Journal for the Theory of Social Behaviour*, vol. 20, no.1, March 1990, by permission of the authors and publisher. The student's essay on pp. 28–34, Poststructuralism as a map through a crisis, is reproduced by permission of the author. Quotations on pp. 36–9 are reproduced from Verena Andermatt Conley, *Hélène Cixous: Writing the Feminine*, exp. edn, University of Nebraska Press, Lincoln, Nebr., 1991, pp. 19, 25–6, 33, 52, 59, 98 & 158, by permission of the University of Nebraska Press; © 1984 by the University of Nebraska Press. The quotation on p. 48 is reproduced from Elizabeth Grosz, Refiguring lesbian desire, unpublished paper, Monash University, 1992, by permission. The quotation on p. 101 is reproduced from the video cover of *Pretty Woman*, Buena Vista Home Video, Burbank, Calif. *Grave Fairytale* on pp. 120–1 is reproduced from *Dorothy Hewett: Selected Poems*, Fremantle Arts Centre Press, Fremantle, WA, 1991, pp. 50–1, by permission of the author and publisher.

Biographical information

Bronwyn Davies is a Professor in the School of Education at James Cook University, Townsville, Qld. Her previous books include *Shards of Glass: Children Reading and Writing beyond Gendered Identities* (Allen & Unwin, Sydney, 1993), *Guidelines for the Elimination of Gender Stereotyping in Primary School Text Books* (Commonwealth Secretariat, London, 1993), *Frogs and Snails and Feminist Tales: Preschool Children and Gender* (Allen & Unwin, Sydney, 1989), and *Life in the Classroom and Playground: The Accounts of Primary School Children* (Routledge & Kegan Paul, London, 1982).

Transcript notation

( )	*author's or observer's comment or observation*
( )	unclear talk
don't	raised voice
/	interruption
-	self-interruption or break in flow of sentence
?	interrogative or upward intonation
. . .	material deleted
slo:ow	sound extended
UPPER	reading from text
T	teacher
S(s)	unidentified student(s)
M	male student
F	female student
(was)	best guess for words spoken

Contents

Chapter 1
Poststructuralist theory, gender and teaching

Poststructuralist theory has opened up exciting new ways of analysing the processes whereby we become gendered. Through an analysis of discursive practices (that is, of the ways we each speak ourselves and each other into existence through our everyday talk), we can discover why it is that the dualistic gender order is so intractable and yet also how we might begin to dismantle it. In this book I set out to make the rather complex field of poststructuralist theory more accessible than it usually is and to show how it might be used to make sense of classroom practices and of classroom texts and talk. The major task of this first chapter is to introduce you to poststructuralist theory.

There are a number of contradictory discourses about what we might want in classrooms in relation to gender. The discourse most widely accepted and used is organised around the concept of equity, implying a *liberal feminist* approach in which we endeavour to establish the right of access for girls to male ways of being, or, at least, to the choices that males would make. But both masculinity and the phallocentric gender order are now seen as problematic. Theories of gender these days tend to stress difference not just between males and females but amongst them. Policies appearing to advocate the sameness of one group to another are beginning to be seen as unacceptable. Many policy writers have substituted the word justice for equity to avoid this assumption of a press towards sameness (that is towards being white, male, heterosexual), but it remains to be seen whether the way principles of justice are understood will entail the same problems. A less widely recognised discourse, sometimes subsumed under the equity discourse, is the *radical feminist* discourse, which advocates that we endeavour to give girls the freedom to be girls and not to see this as a lesser way of being.

Both the liberal feminist and the radical feminist approach are highly problematic. The first leaves unquestioned the value accorded to maleness in the current gender order. It assumes that girls will be all right if they cease being like girls, completely ignoring the complex problems faced by girls and women who do make 'male' choices. The second assumes that if girls value their own femininity they will be able to counteract the enormous weight of the gender order in which masculinity is in the ascendant. It also tends to ignore the extent to which we would have to change curriculum and school texts and talk if we were to give girls an education in which femaleness/femininity was consistently or even predominantly valorised. Furthermore, just what such valorisation would mean is difficult to say, given the complex relation between femaleness and feminism. As Gordon says:

> Female and feminist consciousness stand in a complex relation to each other: clearly they overlap, for the female is the basis of the feminist, yet the

1

feminist arises also out of a desire to escape the female. That seems to me an inescapable tension.

(Gordon in de Lauretis 1986, p. 30)

Those tensions lie in our simultaneous embeddedness in the present and its constructions of masculinity and femininity and our envisaging of a future in which gender is done differently. While the masculine is ascendant and powerful, girls should have access to it. While the feminine is marginalised and downgraded, that marginalisation and downgrading should be counteracted.

To move beyond these tensions and traps, each being inevitable in the current phallocentric gender order, we need to begin the task of deconstructing and so moving beyond masculinity and femininity, maleness and femaleness. We need to find some way in which we might constitute ourselves and our students in ways not tied to the genitals we happen to have. This raises questions about how we can move beyond the dualistic gender order when we don't yet know how to catch ourselves in the act of constituting ourselves and our desire inside the very categories we want to move beyond. It is to poststructuralist theory that we can turn to find ways of both seeing how we are constituted and envisaging ways of moving beyond those constituted patterns of being and desire. This chapter, then, is devoted to introducing you to poststructuralist theory. It does so not with me as an 'authority' who will teach you to think as I do. I write the book from the point of view of one who, like any other, has interacted with poststructuralist texts, made my own sense of them and acquired a new and (for me) empowering way of viewing the events in my everyday world. I use that everyday world and my embeddedness in it to make sense of the texts I read, and I will draw on it here to elaborate what poststructuralist theory means to me.

Poststructuralist theory makes it possible to see the multiple discourses in which we are each inevitably and contradictorily caught up, including discourses of gender. Given that we are all inevitably tied up in patterns of talk and ways of being that constitute us as male or female, poststructuralist theory allows us to think for the moment, holding on to these categories of masculinity and femininity in order to do the valorising work made relevant by radical feminism and to notice and address the exclusions that liberal feminist discourse makes visible. We can do this at the same time as we develop our awareness of the limitations and the powerful entrapments entailed in the categories. And precisely because of those limitations, we can learn both to hold on to and begin the work of abandoning the categories at the same time, to put them *sous rature* or under erasure, as Derrida would say.

The first step in deconstruction, or putting concepts under erasure, is to locate their metaphysical or constructed nature:

Derrida labels as 'metaphysical' any thought-system which depends on an unassailable foundation, a first principle or unimpeachable ground upon which a whole hierarchy of meanings may be constructed. If you examine such principles closely, you can see that they may always be deconstructed. First principles of this kind are commonly defined by what they exclude, by a sort of 'binary opposition'. Deconstruction is the name given to a critical operation by which such oppositions can be partially undermined.

(Sarup 1988, p. 40)

2

In coming to see male and female as constructed binary categories, we discover the way in which they take their meaning through the exclusion of the other. Moving beyond the binary construction involves first valorising and seeing the relevance of the second term for the first. This is followed by the multiplication of categories through a practice of imagining oneself in both categories and also in neither:

> While impossible to freeze conceptually, deconstruction can be broken down into three steps: 1) identify the binaries, the oppositions that structure an argument; 2) reverse/displace the dependent term from its negative position to a place that locates it as the very condition of the positive term; and 3) create a more fluid and less coercive conceptual organisation of terms which transcends binary logic by simultaneously being both and neither of the binary terms.
>
> (Lather 1991, p. 13, drawing on Grosz 1989, p.xv)[1]

Subjectivity

An individual's subjectivity is made possible through the discourses s/he has access to, through a life history of being in the world. It is possible for each of us as teachers and students to research the process of subjectification in order to see its effect on us and on the learning environments we collaboratively produce. The research traditions that most of us are all too familiar with require the removal of 'subjectivity' from any research endeavour, as if objective truths could be established in this way. Once we have understood the constitutive force of discourse, however, and with it the fact that we are all constituted through much the same array of discourses, then the detailed ways in which any one person experiences being a person can be examined, not just to see what the specificity of that person is, but to see the common threads through which being a person, or being male, or being female—or white or black—is accomplished. Examining any individual's subjectivity is thus a way of gaining access to the constitutive effects of the discursive practices through which we are all constituted as subjects and through which the world we all live in is made real. *Our (liberal humanist) belief that we are the architects of our own consciousness and our consciences is as much the result of discourses we have been subjected to (constituted by) as anything else.*

The concept of subjectivity is different from the concept of identity (Davies 1993). It shifts attention away from the unitary non-contradictory selves that we each struggle after as a result of our immersion in humanist discourses and focuses on the shifting, fragmented, multi-faceted and contradictory nature of our experiences. It enables us to see the diversity and richness of our experience of being a person as we find ourselves positioned now one way and now another, inside one set of power relations or another, constituted through one discourse or another, in one context or another. Our subjectivity is in part the result of our particular life histories of being in the world. But our experiences of that life history—even the life history itself and how it unfolds and is told—are the result of intersections of

---

[1] These deconstructive steps have a fascinating similarity to the stages of feminism we have gone through and are still going through; radical feminism parallelling stage 2 and poststructuralist feminism stage 3.

3

discourses, storylines and relations of power.[2] While not negating the power of the conscious and unconscious minds to store and use the multiple layers of knowing that accumulate in any one life, each person is, nevertheless, also in an important sense constituted afresh in each new context, each new set of relations and positionings within discourses and storylines. We are positioned and position ourselves moment by moment as we make our way through the everyday world. In my preschool study I found many examples of the children positioning themselves in terms of their gender.

Joanne, a four-year-old, was not at all happy with the storylines available to girls. She enjoyed the kinds of games that the 'macho' group of boys engaged in—fairly dominant powerful, controlling kinds of games, and she wanted access to those games, not as the female, the *other* to their male, but as one of them, the heroes of their play. At the same time she was extremely socially competent and never in any doubt that she was obliged to achieve herself as identifiably female. She moved competently and strongly, like a boy, but to prevent people mistaking her for a boy she tied her hair up in a girlish topknot. The boys would not often give her access to their games in the way she wanted. Once, when they were playing Voltron, a popular television show at that time, they had let her be the leader and she had had a wonderful time, but mostly they insisted she be the princess (the one who keeps falling off Voltron, becoming victim to the baddies and needing to be saved), and so she refused to join their play.

One occasion when Joanne had access to a powerful position in her play involved the appearance of a new treehouse in the school yard. On that day, there was a hive of excited activity around the new tree house. There were those who could competently climb up the ladder and those who needed to be shown how. There was a feeling of tension and excitement in being up there as the children began figuring how to use this exciting new space. There were several attempts to take possession of the tree house— one forceful attempt on the part of some of the boys in which the teacher intervened. At one point Joanne and her friend Tony began to control who could and could not come up. They had found a technique for preventing people from climbing up the ladder—dropping sawdust, which had been left by the carpenters on the floor of the treehouse, into the tentative, upward-looking faces of the people who were attempting to climb up the ladder. They were deeply immersed in the power and excitement of this takeover of this highly desirable public space. Then Joanne saw me watching and she saw herself through what she imagined were my eyes and she said 'I'm just cleaning the floor, there's all this sawdust here.'

Whether this was simply 'a story', or whether Joanne believed her description of what she was doing, is not really important. What is important is that she knew the correct, domestic narrative into which her activity *should* fit.

---

[2] This process is brilliantly illustrated in Margaret Atwood's short story 'The bog man' (Atwood 1992). The story involves a multiple telling of a romantic relationship, first by the young student who is involved with her professor, that telling being overlayed with the successive tellings of the story as she becomes older. The shifts in who the professor is in each telling reveal precisely the way in which power relations, context and discourses are relevant in the constitution of persons.

Tony, in contrast, and like the group of macho boys displayed an intense and undivided attention to the task of taking over the new territory. There was no hesitation, no visible question about the defensibility of their strategy for establishing their territory, and no need to explain to me, therefore, that they were 'really' innocent. There was no sense of guilt to be explained away. Although Joanne was still able to proceed with the activity there was some hesitation, some experience of doubt about the legitimacy of her forceful, dominant action. She could not be, as Tony appeared to be, fully immersed in asserting herself in this way, at least while I was watching.

(Davies 1990a, p. 507)

Thus we learn to see and to organise our subjectivity in relation to the discourses about what it means to be gendered. The way gender is discursively constituted, and lived as our own experience of ourselves, makes power problematic for those assigned to the female gender. This is not a rational, analysable experience on Joanne's part. Rather, it is 'taking herself up', locating and knowing herself inside the gender order, that is an order in which power and femaleness do not belong together. The subjectivity made possible through gendered storylines is not just used to constitute individual gendered identities, but creates an interpretive lens through which we see the social world. This idea will be explored in detail in chapter three.

Looking at text and at binary forms of thought

In the next chapter I will look at the different discourses that are used to organise the life world of a primary school classroom. This will be done, first, through looking at the way the teacher *talks about* what he does—at the discourses he draws on to make sense of his practice. Then we will look at the discursive practices in his classroom. In looking at discourses or discursive practices *as they are used* in the classroom scene, it will be possible to see the way in which the social structure, power relations, the different positions of each of the participants, the life histories and desires of each individual are made 'real' through the discourses that are used by the participants in this particular setting.

These two ways of looking at discourses are also the ways you might look at this text I am writing. I will pause often to talk about what I am doing, to tell you that I am doing a poststructuralist analysis and to define key words from poststructuralist discourse. In order to understand 'discourse' as it is used here, for example, you can look at what I *say about* discourse (as I will do later) and also at *what I am doing*, what practical use of the word 'discourse' I make. A common way of distinguishing between these two ways of knowing is to say that one is 'abstract', the latter more 'concrete'. Another is to say that one is the 'signifier' and the other the 'signified'. In our education systems we tend to valorise abstraction as a higher, purer form of knowing, to treat it as if it is separate from the concrete while at the same time being a tool with which to analyse and describe the concrete. Or sometimes we see the concrete merely as a path to the more valued abstraction—the form of words, the signifiers that name the world. Abstraction is associated with masculinity and the hard sciences.[3] The capacity to think abstractly is empowering because it has cultural capital, but it can also be a violence to the capacity to know the detail of one's own lived experience independently of the constitutive force of those abstractions. This is particularly so because abstract and concrete are understood as binary opposites rather than inseparable elements of the same thing. Further, it is so when the abstractions themselves are organised in binary terms. An example of this is explored in *Shards of Glass: Children Reading and Writing Beyond Gendered Identities* (Davies 1993). Zac was one of the students in the primary school children and gender project that is reported there. In that study the children were given access to some aspects of poststructuralist theory. The photographic project was part of enabling them to see and read texts of their own lives as gendered texts. Chas Banks was the researcher who undertook the work with these primary school study groups:

> A ... violence experienced by both [male and female students] is achieving the ability to see in simplistic binarisms—to squeeze the multiplicity and variability of everyday life into the binary categories through which school learning is done. Zac, for example, having learned to think in terms of the male–female dualism in which men belong outside in the public world of work and women inside, in domestic scenes, creates this division in his photographic project. His mother is represented as inside and his father as outside the house. As he arranges the photographs, he further establishes this difference by grouping the photos of his mother in the middle of the display poster, with the photos of his father outside, around the outer edges, making the outer boundary of the text he is creating. Chas's questioning reveals something quite other than this binary spatial division between his parents. When he sees this, he explains that it *would* be the way it ought to be, that is the male–female dualism would be being lived out correctly, if circumstances were different. The following conversation takes up where Zac has just explained that his mother doesn't 'really' play cricket, she only 'tries':

> ZAC: ... she does try, she tries playing cricket or soccer or hockey and we play all them out the back/
>
> CHAS: Mm/
>
> ZAC: garden
>
> CHAS: Do you play games with your dad? Does he ever play with you?
>
> ZAC: Oh he usually, he doesn't now 'cause he's always usually working but and he's getting older and but he

---

[3] Note the interesting metaphor, 'hard', associated with male genitalia, an association which discursively creates and maintains an association between 'male', 'abstract' and higher or good or more valued forms of knowledge. We use such metaphors without even noticing what associations are being achieved. We tend to think of metaphors, if we think of them at all, as just a way of talking. But one way in which the world is made to seem inevitable and real is through the unquestioned, unexamined use of everyday words (Lakoff & Johnson 1980).

6

used to muck around with soccer and play cricket. He still plays cricket, his grandfather was A-Grade and he used to play for Dungowan and everything

CHAS: Really?

ZAC: He teaches me strokes and everything

CHAS: Right, but he spends quite a lot of his time working and earning money to keep the house repayments up ((referring back to an earlier conversation)) and/

ZAC: Yeah/

CHAS: and that sort of stuff. And your mum stays at home does she?

ZAC: Yeah

CHAS: But she's looking for a job

ZAC: Oh she isn't really now

CHAS: Has she always stayed at home?

ZAC: Yep

CHAS: She has?

ZAC: Oh when we were young, about 1, 2, 3 she used, she worked at a stock station agents

CHAS: Mm. Notice that these shots of your dad are outside/

ZAC: Yeah/

CHAS: and these ones of your mum are inside. Is that fairly typical of the way they operate?

ZAC: Yep

CHAS: It is?

ZAC: Oh but mum really, usually does help outside with the garden, she does the gardening a lot

CHAS: Does she?

ZAC: Yeah

CHAS: Does she do the flower part of the garden or the vegetable part or/

ZAC: All

CHAS: She does all of it does she?

ZAC: She mows, and does things

CHAS: Right, so she's very capable

ZAC:	Yep
CHAS:	Do you get on well with your mum?
ZAC:	Yeah
CHAS:	Are you as close to your mum, closer to your mum or closer to your dad do you reckon?
ZAC:	Oh, (I'd be) closer to dad if he was at home more probably
CHAS:	Would you?
ZAC:	Yeah
CHAS:	Why do you think that is?
ZAC:	Oh because I like working outside on cars and that sort of thing. Not really sitting inside doing nothing

(Karobran Public, Zac's interview)

Despite all these details of his mother's outside activity, her 'attempts' to play cricket, Zac still sees her as a boring inside person. He is closer to the idea of his (absent) father with whom he can share (the idea of) being male. It is significant that he has come to *like* what he perceives (idealises) as his father's activity. He has learned to desire what his father would be doing if his father were there and not to desire (or even to count as relevant) what his mother ul is doing in his father's absence. Despite his mother's presence and the fact that she does everything, she is the unimportant background to the important figure of the father in Zac's world. The father is held in the foreground, despite his absence. Through this binary or dualistic thinking, Zac actually perceives his mother in terms of absence and lack of significance despite her presence. ('Oh, (I'd be) closer to dad if he was at home more probably... because I like working outside on cars and that sort of thing. Not really sitting inside doing nothing'). The binarism has been taken on as his own, both as a way of telling about the world and as a way of feeling and of positioning himself in relation to the world and of knowing his own maleness. As well, the privileging of the abstract over lived experience, so common an aspect of male thought, is visibly achieved. Although this binary thinking does a violence to the detail of Zac's life, it also privileges him in its achieving of the male as the ascendant or foregrounded element of the dualism.

(Davies 1993, pp. 53–5)

Poststructuralism has begun to disrupt and deconstruct the binarisms through which we structure our knowledge of ourselves and the social world. Binary thought is absolutely fundamental to the maintenance of the male/female dualism. Obviously it is not just male and female alone that are understood in binary terms. There are a whole range of binarisms that are created in the discourses we have access to, many of which are linked to what we understand as male and female.

Wilshire provides the following table of the binary metaphors associated with maleness and femaleness as she discovers them in traditional myths. These stories, which permeate our culture, inform and shape not only the ways in which we

8

understand the concepts male and female but also the storylines through which we take ourselves up as one or the other:

KNOWLEDGE (accepted wisdom) / IGNORANCE (the occult and taboo)

higher (up) / lower (down)

good, positive / negative, bad

mind (ideas), head, spirit / body (flesh), womb (blood), Nature (Earth)

reason (the rational) / emotions and feelings (the irrational)

cool / hot

order / chaos

control / letting be, allowing, spontaneity

objective (outside, 'out there') / subjective (inside, immanent)

literal truth, fact / poetic truth, metaphor, art

goals / process

light / darkness

written text, Logos / oral tradition, enactment, Myth

Apollo as sky-sun / Sophia as earth-cave-moon

public sphere / private sphere

seeing, detached / listening, attached

secular / holy and sacred

linear / cyclical

permanence, ideal (fixed) forms / change, fluctuations, evolution

'changeless and immortal' / process, ephemeras (performance)

hard / soft

independent, individual, isolated / dependent, social, interconnected, shared

dualistic / whole

MALE / FEMALE

(Wilshire 1989, pp. 95–6)

I find this a particularly fascinating table. I can read down the righthand column and resonate with many of the terms, seeing in some how I take myself to be, as woman, some how I would ideally like to be and others as I know I should be. A few I reject altogether. But as a whole they make a highly recognisable set of concepts through which femaleness is understood in the stories, both lived and imagined, of our culture. But when I look at the lefthand column, I also recognise something of myself there, particularly the self I have acquired through being educated, through learning to be an academic and a writer. At the same time I recognise in the lefthand column the ideas and ideals of maleness as we construct that within our culture. And there are many men who are recognisable as having qualities from the righthand column. This double visioning is important since it reveals the way in which we can hold intact the idea of maleness and femaleness as binary opposites, even recognise ourselves in that division, at the same time as we can enumerate many examples of transgressions, movement outside the binary division. Our capacity to do so is at least in part the result of discursive strategies we have learned at school (Baker & Davies 1989).

9

As long as we are capable of holding the binarisms intact, there is always precisely the risk that those ways of being that threaten or disrupt the binarism will be understood as transgressive, rather than as, say, a multiplicity to be celebrated.

Being a person (rather than being male or female) actually involves both sides of the table. To the extent that men see themselves as persons they encompass both sides. To the extent that they see themselves as heroic or god-like, at least within the Christian tradition, they will struggle towards the lefthand side, away from the feminine. And, as I have pointed out in *Shards of Glass*, it is fundamental to masculinity that one achieve some kind of heroic status to be successfully male. Thus the table needs to be understood as process rather than stasis. The boy/man struggles away from the feminine (either the feminine ideal or actual female persons) in an attempt to become not what they are. The feminine thus becomes the other that one struggles not to be like. It is the negative form against which one defines what it is to have achieved (male) personhood. The girl/woman learns the qualities of maleness through her education and her access to the public sphere, but always with the proviso that she not compromise her femininity, that she remain true to the female side of the binary divide. This particular split has been the subject of many an educated woman's struggle (Walkerdine 1989).

The struggle of girls and women to be heroic, to disrupt the automatic association between maleness and the 'superior', culturally dominant forms are understandably rejected by boys and men since they undermine the binary base on which the achievement of (male) personhood rests. This rejection was painfully evident in much of the work Chas did with the primary school study groups. The boys sexualised the female characters in the fictions they read and wrote and they sexualised the girls in their interactions with them. This was most evident when girls stepped outside their 'proper' feminine place, that is, when they presumed that they too could have access to the heroic. A conversation that reveals this kind of resistance I have analysed in *Shards of Glass* as follows:

> . . . Chas and the Karobran study group were attempting to construct a resistive storyline in which they did not fall into patterns dictated by the dominant discourses on masculinity and femininity. Or, more correctly, Chas and Rosie are attempting to do so. The boys are resisting this shift and using the story as an opportunity to assert male power and control over girls/women. While assenting to the fact that there must be a female hero, they find a number of ways to increase their own heroism and the heroism of the males in the story by gaining various forms of ascendancy over the females in the story and over the female story tellers. The group has been discussing what the story is to be about. All want something exciting, to do with danger, murder and mystery. The transcript begins with a struggle on the part of the boys to import rape into the storyline and to connect it to the murder of the rape victim (13). They manage to do this by claiming that they want 'fun' (3) and equality (7–15), that is, there will be both a male and a female victim, so they will be equal/the same. This is a ruse, however, as they are quite clear that the female is to be the 'real' victim (20, 22). Rosie accepts that there must be a victim as she cannot imagine a story without one (17) but she attempts to develop the fun/equality combination by removing the rape (23, 24, 28). She is overruled by the boys and Anna who insist on rape (26, 27, 29):

1 MAL:	I've got one, um rape and murder and sex and fun and mystery all together sort of thing, know what I mean? Like there's these people they sort of have sex/
2 BRIAN:	Mystery that's boring
3 MAL:	it's fun then one of the people want to have sex with a boy so he rapes her and murders her and then it's a mystery to solve it
4 ANNA:	Rape murder, sex and fun ...
5 KEN	I'd like to do what Mal said...
6 CHAS:	Now Brian, remember how we're doing a story that completely resists all the dominant discourses here and we're going to develop a storyline that resists the dominant story lines, we're not going to/
7 KEN:	'cause they are both victims
8 CHAS	Well you'll have to do it in terms of the story line. Are we going to have girl as victim?
9 BRIAN:	No
10 ROSIE:	No
11 KEN:	No
12 CHAS:	What are we going to have?
13 BRIAN:	Both
14. MAL:	Both
15 ROSIE:	Both
16 CHAS:	Why do we have to have victims any way?
17 ROSIE:	Because otherwise there'd be no story
18 MAL:	Because it makes it interesting
19 ANNA:	'Cause that's the mystery part of it
20 MAL:	Make it that the girl is the major victim and the guy is just the victim
...	
21 CHAS:	Alright, have you decided you want boy and girl as victim
22 MAL:	Yeah but like the girl is the real victim
23 ROSIE:	No ...

24 ROSIE: They could be having sex and fun and someone
                comes along and murders both of them

. . .

25 CHAS: What are they going to be the victims of?

26 ANNA: Rape and murder

27 MAL: Rape murder

28 ROSIE: No sex and fun because /

29 BRIAN: No rape and murder

                                        (Karobran Public)

Thus the boys manage, by assenting to structural equality between the
victims (it is a male and female victim who are to be murdered, not just a
female) to distract attention from their insertion of the rape into the story,
thus guaranteeing at least one moment of male domination over a female.
Mal knows full well that this makes the girl the 'major victim' (20) or the 'real
victim' (22). With the help of Anna, he manages to overrule Rosie when she
tries to change this to a benign form of sexuality between the two victims
(24, 28). Anna's position is quite different from Mal's and the other boys. ...
she knows the world is a dangerous place for girls/women and does not
believe it possible for women on their own to be heroic. She works at being
a tomboy, cultivating herself as male, wanting heroism for herself, not as
female but as male. At the same time as she wants a non-sexist world, she
works with the boys to hold the male-female dualism in place. This is most
evident in the next part of the conversation which is a discussion about who
is going to be the hero of their story. (They are using the term saviour,
following on from their deconstructive reading of *Snow White*.) They start
with the idea of using the police but then reject that and finally decide on
detectives. Rosie and Chas suggest a female hero (34, 36, 38) but this is
rejected by Anna and Ken. Anna wants a male detective (41) and Ken
suggests they go for equality again by having a male and a female. This is
assented to by Anna on the grounds that the story will not then be sexist.
Rosie valiantly tries to continue the story of the female hero who is a friend
of the victim, weaving in the male detective as someone she hires (50, 52)
but this is regarded as sexist/unequal (53) and so Rosie assents to a male
and female couple who are both detectives.

In the following excerpts they discuss first what the female victim, Lisa, will
look like and then what the detectives will look like:

30 CHAS: Now, generally in the traditional storylines we
                have the male saviour, we're resisting that domi-
                nant storyline so who are we gonna have or
                what's gonna happen, who's gonna be the sav-
                iour in this?

31 KEN: The police

32 ANNA: Why the saviour?

33 CHAS: Save someone/

12

34	ROSIE:	A policewoman, the girl's best friend, a police woman/
35	ANNA:	Can we have something other than that, police this, police that, let's have something different
36	CHAS:	Alright, well the girl's best friend?
37	ANNA:	The guy's a detective/
38	ROSIE:	The girl's best friend found out that she was murdered and she set out to find out who it was so she/
39	ANNA:	No
40	KEN:	No, no
41	ANNA:	A detective
42	CHAS:	Alright, it's a private detective but is it going to be a female or a male private detective? 'Cause usually/
43	KEN:	Both
44	ANNA:	Oh hopefully male
45	ROSIE:	Female
46	ANNA:	Have a lady and a man/
47	KEN/MAL:	Yeah
48	ANNA	'cause then it is not um sexist
49	CHAS:	Alright, put that down, lady and man
50	ROSIE:	But the girl's best friend, she finds she gets a detective/
51	KEN:	Yeah, but then it would be sexist
52	ROSIE:	to come along and they set out to find out what happened to her
53	ANNA:	That'll be sexist if it's only a girl, I reckon there should be two parts, a girl and a boy
54	ROSIE:	Actually the two best friends from the man and the woman can set out. . .
55	CHAS:	Now we're trying to resist the dominant discourse here. How's Lisa ((the female victim)) going to look, what sort of a girl is she going to be
56	KEN:	Sexy
57	CAROLYN:	Pretty

13

58	BRIAN:	Scared
59	CHAS:	Now look if she's sexy and scared and pretty it's like the dominant discourse revisited. We want something totally different
60	ROSIE:	How about this/
61	ANNA:	Fat and ugly
62	ROSIE:	No
63	BRIAN:	Fuckin' ugly!!
64	KEN:	Just ordinary
65	CHAS:	She could be a bit plump, can't she be a bit plump?
66	ROSIE:	Yeah she's chubby
67	ANNA:	Abandoned, abandoned with the car. . .
68	BRIAN:	((said very close to the microphone so it couldn't be heard by the others)) Rosie wants to give Mal a root
69	MAL:	Brian shut up
70	CHAS	What's Wilfred ((the male detective)) like?
71	ANNA:	Dumb, he's big and/
72	ROSIE:	No!
73	KEN:	No big and sexy
74	BRIAN:	He's solid
75	KEN:	Solid
76	MAL:	Solid
77	KEN:	Body building
78	BRIAN:	Heavy built/
79	CHAS:	Alright, solid
80	BRIAN:	heavy built
81	ROSIE:	He could be a boxer
82	KEN:	Like Arnold Schwartznegger, a body builder
83	CHAS:	Now listen you can't have the girl as the whimp then she's got to be just as strong and just as capable as what he is

84 MAL: Big boobs

((laughter))

85 ROSIE: No she could be sexy looking and very rough

86 BRIAN: That's what you are

(Karobran Public)

In developing the character of Lisa they find it difficult to find an alternative to sexy, pretty and scared. If she cannot be these, she must be fat and ugly (61), even 'fuckin' ugly' (63). This aggressive description from Brian is evocative of an attitude I encountered when counselling an adolescent boy involved in gang rape. He explained to me that girls called 'dogs' are regarded as sexually available to anyone and can be forcefully raped if they do not assent to sex, since they do not belong to anyone. At the same time, my own children explained to me that 'dog' is a common term for ugly girls/women. Brian's whispered statement into the microphone that 'Rosie wants to give Mal a root' (68) follows on from the discussion of the 'fuckin' ugly' victim. It also follows Rosie's attempts to create a solitary female hero. She has put herself at risk by positioning herself outside the male–female dualism and their aggressive sexual talk is letting her know it. The description of the male detective creates no such tension. Apart from Anna's suggestion that he is 'dumb' (71) the group smoothly and collaboratively construct an archetypal powerful male, 'like Arnold Schwartznegger' (73–82). When Chas asserts that the female detective has to be just as good as the male detective, Mal immediately sexualizes her by making her the ultra-female other to Arnold S, (84). Rosie assents to the sexuality of the woman, not as sex object, but by asserting that looking sexy is not incompatible with being really rough. This is then turned on her—it is what she is—sexy and rough (86). By association, she is the sexual other to the male hero (Mal/Arnold) and probably at risk of sexual assault.

Girls' heroism and power, their claims to an incorporation of masculinity, are thus made transgressive of their subordinate position to males. Heroism and power are desired and explored by girls, but always undermined, even in the guise of equality. The boys' strategies for undermining the girls are read by the boys as heroic moves against both the girls and the adult women who attempt to control them. Boys' expressions of heroism and power are, in contrast, moves closer towards the male god/adult/hero. While they may well be transgressive of childhood and 'goodness', the very adult women who are adult other to their child and who control definitions of goodness, are the very other against whom they can practice their moves towards the god/ideal. Thus Mal and his mates can disrupt Chas's plan to write a story that undermines the male–female dualism with total equanimity. They can do so while appearing to co-operate and to be enthusiastic about the project. Going back to Mal's statement at the beginning of the last chapter, girls can be equal to boys by being like them, and by striving towards the same male god/ideal. But if given the opportunity he will use them to achieve displays of (masculine) identity by sexualizing them and by using sex to undermine the possibility of their achieving heroic positionings. Masculinity is, after all, competitive, and heterosexuality is fundamental to the maintenance of the hierarchical dualism.

(Davies 1993, pp. 102–107)

15

This conversation amongst the students in the Karobran study group makes starkly evident the fallacy of so much of the equity discourse which assumes that if male and female are equally represented, justice has been achieved. The fact that male and female can still be achieved as opposite with male in the ascendant, despite equal representation, cannot be addressed with silence about difference nor with the pious hope that equal representation will eventually lead to the dismantling of hegemonic masculinity. As long as patterns of desire are constructed in relation to a binary gender order, males will find ways to maintain their ascendancy (Davies 1990a, 1993).

Boys and men are often not conscious of the ways in which their activities are to do with the establishment of their male, dominant position. They perceive their activity, rather, as achieving personhood. This is because within the binary pair of male and female, male is the unmarked category, female the marked. That which is marked is visible as such. That which is unmarked is invisible as such. Because maleness is the unmarked category, and female the marked (Connell 1987), boys and men may not be able to name the fact that who they are and what they want to be is 'masculine', since masculinity and personhood are experienced as synonymous. Kimmel makes an excellent account of the moment at which he discovered this unmarked or invisible feature of masculinity. He was sitting in on a seminar on feminist theory where he witnessed the following confrontation between a white woman and a black woman. He says:

> Their argument centred around the question of whether their similarities as women were greater than their racial differences. The white woman asserted that the fact that they were both women bonded them, despite racial differences. They shared a common oppression as women, and were both 'sisters under the skin'. The black woman disagreed.
>
> 'When you wake up in the morning and look in the mirror, what do you see?' she asked.
>
> 'I see a woman', replied the white woman hopefully.
>
> 'That's precisely the problem', replied the black woman. 'I see a black woman. For me race is visible every minute of the day, because it is how I am *not* privileged in this culture. Race is invisible to you which is why our alliance will always feel false and strained to me.'
>
> When I heard this, I was startled. For when I looked in the mirror, I thought I saw a 'human being', a generic person, universally generalizable. What had been concealed—race, and gender, and class—was suddenly visible. As a middle-class white man, I was able to not think about the ways in which class and race and gender had shaped my existence. Marginality is visible, and painfully visceral. Privilege is invisible, and painlessly pleasant.
>
> (Kimmel 1990, p. 94)

Making discourse visible

Discourse is used in a number of ways, depending on the context in which it is being used. The poststructuralist use of the word is most commonly attributed to Foucault, though Foucault did not invent it. Rather, a community of speakers and writers, of which he was a particularly prolific member, developed a shared understanding of ways that the term could be used to express the ideas they were developing (Foucault 1977). The task of providing the definition, the statement about the way the word is used by a particular author or group of authors, is often accomplished by someone outside their immediate community, but who wants to take up that way of speaking, that discourse, to develop their own ideas. The definition is necessary as a way of making sense to those outside the original community, or not familiar with the way of talking/writing being used by the writer. It can also be a way of establishing authority and credibility by referring to an accepted or recognised authority in the field. Kress's definition of 'discourse' is as follows:

> Institutions and social groupings have specific meanings and values which are articulated in language in *systematic ways*. Following the work particularly of the French philosopher Michel Foucault, I refer to these systematically-organised modes of talking as DISCOURSE. Discourses are systematically-organised sets of statements which give expression to the meanings and values of an institution. Beyond that, they define, describe and delimit what it is possible to say and not possible to say (and by extension—what it is possible to do or not to do) with respect to the area of concern of that institution, whether marginally or centrally. A discourse provides a set of possible statements about a given area, and organises and gives structure to the manner in which a particular topic, object, process is to be talked about. In that it provides descriptions, rules, permissions and prohibitions of social and individual actions.
>
> (Kress 1985, pp. 6–7)

Weedon's (feminist poststructuralist) statement about discourse, while also drawing on Foucault, is different in intriguing ways from Kress's definition:

> Discourses, in Foucault's work, are ways of constituting knowledge, together with the social practices, forms of subjectivity and power relations which inhere in such knowledges and the relations between them. Discourses are more than ways of thinking and producing meaning. They constitute the 'nature' of the body, unconscious and conscious mind and emotional life of the subjects which they seek to govern. Neither the body nor thoughts and feelings have meaning outside their discursive articulation, but the ways in which discourse constitutes the minds and bodies of individuals is always part of a wider network of power relations, often with institutional bases.
>
> (Weedon 1987, p. 108)

By juxtaposing these two definitions it is possible to see the relevance of the *context* of the writing and the *subject positions* imaginatively available to the authors of any text. Kress produces a definition which emphasises the conscious, organised and controlling aspects of discourse. This is not incompatible with his position in the world as male. Weedon, in contrast, while not in disagreement with Kress, is much more focused on those aspects of discourse that take their effect in the lives of actual persons, and so brings the body, emotions and the unconscious mind into the definition of what discourse constitutes. Weedon writes as a *feminist* poststructuralist. She thus writes from the position of one who has heightened her awareness of gender, of her own genderedness and her experience of being female

17

in a world where masculinity and power are closely linked. Power and powerlessness are central to Weedon's definition as is her experience of being constituted through the words of others. Whereas for Kress, the institution is the predominant organising concept in analysing discourse, for Weedon it is an occasional element mentioned at the end of her definition.

Each author's subjectivity—their daily experience of being in the world, of being constituted in and through various discourses in one or another context—is necessarily implicated in their writing. Whereas feminist writers in particular have begun to reveal the detailed contexts out of which they write, many writers (particularly male and particularly writers unfamiliar with poststructuralism) continue to write as if it were possible and even ideal to achieve an 'objective' statement, that is, a statement untouched by, not mediated through the lived experience of the author and the contexts in which they write and in which they are read. The concept of marking is useful in understanding this experience. In binary pairs such as male/ female, heterosexual/homosexual, normal/mad, the first term is ascendant and normative, the second term is a deviation from the norm. In each case the person positioned in the first category need not be aware of their categorisation. They can see themselves simply as a person whom any one else is free to be like. Those in the second part of each pair are aware of themselves as being in that category, their definition of themselves being intricately tied to their category membership. Thus in the case of Kress and Weedon, the positions that they each write from are as unmarked male who can make certain assumptions about power and agency that render them fairly unproblematic, the other as feminist where the marked nature of this category is both lived and analysed. These positions are relevant to the way they take up and use the concept. Foucault, in contrast, wrote both from the unmarked position of (male) person and from the marked position of homosexual. His categorisation as homosexual gave him the experience of being marked and of being powerless and other to hegemonic masculinity (Eribon 1991). His access to the position of unmarked (male) person was thus never guaranteed. His capacity to write at the margins, his awareness of otherness is no doubt due in no small part to that uncertainty.

What I have just done here is to provide a poststructuralist analysis of a poststructuralist term. That is, I have looked at it in terms of who is speaking, from what position, in what context and with what political effect. To thus provide insight into the multiple possible readings of the word 'discourse' is quite different from the more usual provision of an authoritative, abstract definition which holds the meaning in place. This is not to say that the word discourse has no particular meaning within poststructuralist theory, but that any meaning of any word can only be grasped through an awareness of context, of speaker, of political effects and so on. Castor, in discussing Harraway's contribution to this debate says:

> . . . she argues that the ability to see is politicized. 'Vision is *always* a question of the power to see—and perhaps of the violence implicit in our visualizing practices. With whose eyes were my eyes crafted? ... Feminist objectivity is about limited location and situated knowledge, not about

transcendence and splitting of subject and object. It allows us to become answerable for what we learn how to see.' ... [Harraway's] shifted metaphor of the 'objective' view is about being accountable for what and *how* we have the power to see.

(Castor 1991, p. 64)

It is precisely this ability to see that our 'eyes have been crafted', and the political effects of this, that a poststructuralist discourse provides. How gender is created and sustained, in what contexts, within what power relations and with what effects on the minds/bodies of each of us, is something we can begin to make visible to ourselves and to our students in our interactions with them.

Poststructuralist discourse thus calls attention to the unmarked and the invisible in a number of ways. The constitutive power of ways of talking and writing are not usually made visible. Rather, they are usually regarded as the transparent medium through which real worlds are *described and analysed*, real worlds which have their existence independent of the words spoken about them. There are any number of assumptions made about what good science and good social science are that come from the unmarked condition of being a privileged male speaker. People so positioned can make assumptions that can only be made as a member of an elite made up of white, heterosexual, middle-class or upper-class males. They can do so without recognising that that is what they are doing precisely because each of these characteristics is unmarked. Some of the privileges that accrue to white heterosexual upper-class males are thus:

- a certainty about who they are, the importance attaching to their individual being having been made clear to them, and the resources (signs) for developing certainty about it having been made available from birth;

- a certainty about what is true along with an inability to see the truths that inhere in the experiences of the powerless or anyone attempting to call in question the standard, hegemonic truths;

- a blindness to the multiplicity of being that occurs with not being the one who is positioned by others, but rather always being able to position oneself and others as one deems appropriate;

- a blindness to the ways in which being elite and male gives one privilege, this being unmarked in their absolute taken-for-grantedness; and

- a dismissing of passion as detrimental to clear thinking, their certainty of position making passion irrelevant in their claims to power. The result of this is that the passionate attacks of the oppressed on the status quo can be dismissed as the emotional ravings of people not properly educated and without access to reason.

The effects on others of this attitude is a violence naively perpetrated in the name of such valorised concepts as 'science' and 'objectivity'. It leads to the

19

invisibility and silencing of all those in the marginal, non-ascendant groups. As Hanmer argues:

> It is contradictory to argue that politicized inquiry can increase the objectivity of inquiry only if the epistemological stance is a belief that research can be value-free, neutral, without a point of view, objective. This epistemological stance has served men well. It has enabled men to retail their views as the only view, as the knowledge of humankind, and to render women invisible. Only social superordinates can utilize in their favour this way of knowing the world; their so-called objectivity is the emergent quality of their position as social superordinates.
>
> (Hanmer 1990, p. 28)

By making hegemonic sets of assumptions visible, the nature of what we take to be factual or real is profoundly shifted. Far from objectivity being the ideal after which we all strive, it becomes an idea which is on occasion revealed as both misleading and stultifying:

> 'Fact is unstable by its very nature. Narouz once said to me that he loved the desert because there "the wind blew out one's footsteps like candle-flames". So it seems to me does reality. How then can we hunt for the truth?'
>
> (Durrell 1962, p. 278)

> The stereotype is the word repeated without any magic, any enthusiasm, as though it were natural, as though by some miracle this recurring word were adequate on each occasion for different reasons, as though to imitate could no longer be sensed as an imitation ... Nietzsche has observed that 'truth' is only the solidification of old metaphors.
>
> (Barthes 1989, p. 42)

Positioning

Feminist poststructuralist theory thus makes relevant the power of discursive and interactive practices to create and sustain individual subjectivities and social structures and it provides a number of concepts through which an analysis of this process can be undertaken. Fundamental concepts within poststructuralist theory, apart from discourse and its constitutive power, are subject position, positioning and storyline. An interesting example can be drawn from the work McDermott undertook working with reading groups in a first-grade classroom. After videotaping the reading lessons with the 'top' and the 'bottom' reading group and analysing the patterns of movement taking place in each group, McDermott was able to show that the top group were able to use their entire lesson on the task of reading whereas the bottom group spent only half their allocated reading time on the actual task of learning to read. Of the top reading group McDermott says:

> Each of these turns to read or answer the teacher is marked by the members *positioning* each other in a particular way ... Throughout the top group's lesson, the same positioning occurs at the beginning of each turn and lasts until the turn is over. Then the members orient to the turn change by shifting their bodies and attention to the teacher or the next person to

read. And then they shift back into the reading positioning. Thus, the flow of behaviour is turn positioning, juncture, turn positioning, juncture, and so on.

He goes on to say:

> ... the maintenance of a line of action takes work on the part of all the participants to that action. A speaker cannot maintain a positioning without the help of a listener. A teacher cannot maintain the positioning of a teacher without the help of students, and so on... the people in an interaction, speakers and listeners, teachers and students, take on characteristic postures at the same time, in concert with one another. In this way, people are each other's contexts in that they form an environment for each other about the reality of that environment for each other and offer feedback to each other.

> (McDermott 1976, pp. 94–5)

The subject position 'good reader' was thus made available to the top group because that was the context they created for each other. The teacher would sit with the group in a physically closed circle, each child 'carpentered' to the desk, their attention focused entirely on the books in front of them (figure 1). The turns would pass straightforwardly around the group so that no time was taken on bidding for a turn, and each child knew which passage to anticipate and could therefore rehearse it while waiting for their turn. In contrast, the subject position 'slow reader' was created by an entirely different set of strategies on the part of teacher and students. Here, the teacher invites the students to bid for turns, not wanting them to have to attempt passages they can't manage. The closed carpentering and the predictability of the top group is thus absent. During bidding time the group becomes interruptable by other students and by the teacher herself as she looks up around the classroom to note what other (higher status) students are doing (figure 2). When the teacher actually leaves the group to attend to those other students the group engages in 'anarchy' which can be read as a strategy to bring the teacher back on task (figure 3). The storyline or discourse that says that, in contrast to good readers, slow readers must not be embarrassed by being asked to read passages that are too difficult, thus leads the participants to create a context in which the subject position 'good reader' positions students in such a way that their chances of learning are maximised, while the subject position 'slow reader' positions students in such a way that their chances of learning are minimised. I have further analysed this 'interruptability' of 'poor students' in Davies and Munro (1987).

Figure 1   Reading positioning Ia: Looking at the book

Figure 2   Procedural positioning IIa: Getting-a-turn to read

Figure 3   Waiting positioning IV: Waiting for the teacher

Positioning also takes place through ways of speaking-as-usual that may be equally unexamined by the speakers. In order to illustrate this point I will use a story taken from an article written with Harré. In this article we argue for using the concept of 'positioning' rather than 'role' to show the way in which discourses open up, or make possible, certain subject positions through and in terms of which we interact with the world. Whereas role is somehow external to the person, something that can be taken up or put aside (the 'real' person presumably remaining separate from those various roles), we argue in that paper that there is no self independent of the positions through which we each fabricate our selves and are fabricated. Position is a much more fluid concept than role and recognises the constitutive force of discourse to make/fabricate the stories or narratives through which meaningful lives are made.[4]

> In our story we have called ourselves Sano and Enfermada. Sano and Enfermada are, at the point the story begins, at a conference. It is a winter's day in a strange city and they are looking for a chemist's shop to try to buy some medicine for Enfermada. A subzero wind blows down the long street. Enfermada suggests they ask for directions rather than conducting a random search. Sano, as befits the one in good health, and accompanied by Enfermada, darts into shops to make enquiries. After some time it becomes clear that there is no such shop in the neighbourhood and they agree to call a halt to their search. Sano then says 'I'm sorry to have dragged you all this way when you're not well'. His choice of words surprises Enfermada who replies 'You didn't drag me, I chose to come', occasioning some surprise in turn to Sano.
>
> ... The subsequent debate between our protagonists ran as follows:
>
> Sano protests that he feels responsible and Enfermada protests in return that she does not wish him to feel responsible since that places her in the position of one who is not responsible, and by implication, that she is one who is incapable of making decisions about her own well being. They then debate whether one taking responsibility deprives the other of responsibility. For Sano the network of obligations is paramount. He is at first unable to grasp the idea that anyone could suppose that the fulfilment of a taken-for-granted obligation on the healthy to take charge of the care of the ill could be construed as a threat to some freedom that he finds mythical. Enfermada is determined to refuse Sano's claim of responsibility, since in her feminist framework it is both unacceptable for another to position her as merely an accessory to their actions, rather than someone who has

---

[4] In quoting at length from this paper, I am, in an important sense, interrupting my own narrative. One of the features of poststructuralist theory is that one makes visible the intertextuality of any text, that is the way in which one text is necessarily an interweaving of many texts. That interweaving is generally made invisible, the voice of the author maintaining the control and the flow of ideas. By inserting large chunks of other texts, I rob you, as reader, of the illusion of a smooth flow. At the same time I make the presence of the authorial voice more visible by the simple act of interrupting it. I thus remind you of the constructed nature of the text you are reading. The footnotes littered throughout the text are a similar device. Sometimes I use them to comment on what I am saying—to invite you to stand for the moment outside the linear flow and to see what is going on from another point of view. They are also another attempt to specify the complexity of the knowledges being explored.

agency in her own right, *and* for her to accept such a positioning. Her concern is only in part for the unintended subject position that his words have apparently invited her to step into. She believes that his capacity to formulate their activity in such a way may be indicative of a general attitude towards her (and to women in general) as marginal, as other than central actors in their own life stories. She knows that he does not wish or intend to marginalise women and so she draws attention to the subject position made available in his talk and refuses to step into it. But her protest positions Sano as sexist, a positioning which he in turn finds offensive. His inclination is therefore to reject Enfermada's gloss as an incorrect reading of his words. But this of course only makes sense in his moral order of interpersonal obligations, not in the feminist moral order. Both speakers are committed to a pre-existing idea of themselves that they had prior to the interchange, Enfermada as a feminist and Sano as one who wishes to fulfil socially mandatory obligations. They are also both committed to their hearing of the interchange. Their protests are each aimed at sustaining these definitions and as such have strong emotional loading.

The episode went through a number of further cycles of reciprocal offence … One of them involved Sano in accusing Enfermada of working off a worst interpretation principle which he claims is characteristic of the kind of ultra-sensitive response that feminists and members of minority groups engage in when responding to 'fancied slights'. Enfermada hears this as a claim that she is unnecessarily making life difficult for herself, alienating people (presumably including Sano) from her and her feminist views. This bothers Enfermada more than the original 'apology' because she sees herself not only robbed of agency but as trivialised and silly, an objectionable member of a minority group who, if they behaved properly, could have equitable membership of society along with Sano. The whole point of her original protest was that his words robbed her of access to that equitable world whether he intended it or not. Until that point she had believed that his intentions were in fact good, which was why it was worth raising the issue. Now she sees that even knowing how upsetting it is to be so positioned in his narrative, his wish is to allocate all responsibility for inequitable treatment that she receives to her own personal style…

There are several further points to be made in relation to this analysis.

It shows the way in which two people can be living quite different narratives without realising that they are doing so. In the absence of any protest on Enfermada's part, Sano need never have questioned how his position as care giver would appear in the moral order of someone whose position was radically different from his. Without her particular reply he could not have realised that he could be heard as paternalistic. Her silence could only act as confirmation of his moral order.

Words themselves do not carry meaning. Sano's use of the apology-format is ambiguous. When it is placed in the context of Enfermada's narrative it causes indexical offence. Similarly, her protest at being 'made helpless' disturbs him since, in his story, it denies what he takes to be a ubiquitous moral obligation.

We have shown the relational nature of positioning—that is, in Enfermada's moral order, one who takes themselves up as responsible for joint lines of action, may position the other as not responsible. Or if one takes up the position of being aggrieved in relation to another then the other is a perpetrator of the injustice. We have shown that what seems obvious from one position, and readily available to any other person who would only behave or interpret in the correct way, is not necessarily so for the person in the 'other' position. The relative nature of positions not only to each other but to moral orders can make the perception of one almost impossible for the other, in the relational position, to grasp.

One's beliefs about the sorts of persons, including oneself, who are engaged in a conversation are central to how one understands what has been said. Exactly what is the force of any utterance on a particular occasion will depend on that understanding.

In demonstrating the shifting nature of positions, depending on the narrative/metaphors/images through which the positioning is being constituted, we have shown how both the social act performed by the uttering of those words and the effect that action has is a function of the narratives employed by each speaker as well as the particular positions that each speaker perceives the other speaker to be taking up.

There are normative expectations at each level. Sano is surprised at Enfermada's protest because according to conventions of the nurse-patient narrative, there is a normative expectation that the poorly both need and accept care. Of course this narrative also includes the case of the difficult patient. Enfermada for her part is accustomed to being marginalised in men's talk. In hearing him as giving offence she is interpreting him as engaging in normative male behaviour. And of course within this narrative men are notoriously unable to recognise the ways in which their taking up of paternalistic positions negates the agency of the women they are interacting with.

We have shown the necessity of separating out intended meanings from hearable meanings in the process of developing discursive practices that are not paternalistic or discriminatory *in their effect*. The (personal) political implications of attending to the discursive practices through which one positions oneself and is positioned, are that one's speech-as-usual with its embedded metaphors, images, forms, etc., can be recognised as inappropriate to personal/political beliefs both of one's own and of others with whom one interacts.

(Davies & Harré 1990, pp. 55–8)[5]

There is no doubt that integral to the argument between Sano and Enfermada was an attempt on the part of each to convince the other that the perspective from

---

[5] An aspect of the interchange not analysed in this paper with Harré, which I find to be a curious omission, is the metaphorical loading of the term 'dragged'—'I'm sorry I have dragged you'. It seems so obviously to evoke cave-man images that it could well be central to Enfermada's refusal of Sano's words. It is possible that Enfermada was aware that Sano would see such an analysis as so outrageous that his ability to see her as having any claim to be listened to would have vanished altogether. In other words, what is sayable is dependent not only on what is hearable by the others in any particular social scene but also on what is hearable as credible and reasonable. Another interesting feature of the text of Sano and Enfermada is the choice of names, Sano being Spanish for (masculine) healthy and Enfermada Spanish for (feminine) sick. Of course, Sano chose the names, thus using a subtle textual device to assert his reading of the situation as the real one. This could be construed as an act of patriarchal naming—controlling through words.

which they viewed the interaction was the 'correct' perspective. Each wanted not only to make sense for themselves in terms of the discourses in which they had invested themselves but to make that the sense that the other took up. There are two elements of this insistence. One is the investment each had made in their own idea of who they were and their refusal to have the other position them in ways that undermined that idea. The other is an investment in a particular discourse as a means of interpreting oneself and the social world. The validity of one's interpretations, of the sense-making one is engaged in, depend upon being able to bring one's interpretive schemes to bear on a range of events.

Seeing with poststructuralist eyes

My intention in elaborating feminist poststructuralist theory in relation to education as I am doing here, or in teaching my own students, is not to colonise or impose. It is to enable the participants to have a different way of seeing that does not necessarily replace other ways of seeing, but enables the student and the teacher to *position themselves differently* in relation to existing discourses. That different positioning gives the student a position of power in relation to existing discourses which is additional to the power gained through being able to use existing discourses competently. That power comes from being able to see the effects of discourses upon those who are constituted through them.

There is a sense in which we all attempt to *colonise* the world with the discourses we have taken up as our own, and through which we have been constituted. Kress comments that discourses tend to colonise surrounding areas not of immediate concern to them, to interpret aspects of other institutions in their own terms:

> Discourses tend towards exhaustiveness and inclusiveness; that is, they attempt to account not only for an area of immediate concern to an institution, but attempt to account for increasingly wider areas of concern. ... A metaphor which I use to explain the effects of discourse to myself is that of a military power whose response to border skirmishes is to occupy the adjacent territory. As problems continue, more territory is occupied, then settled and colonised. A discourse colonises the social world imperialistically, from the point of view of one institution.
>
> (Kress 1985, p. 7)

But Kress's analysis of colonisation removes the discourse from the speakers, from the lived experience of being a speaker, subjected to the constitutive force of discourse. His metaphor is of war, not of the kind lived and fought by soldiers or suffered by civilians, but of the kind envisaged by political leaders and as reported in the media and in recorded in history books, that is in terms of borders and territories and political power. Within the combat metaphor, any discourse is violent and has the potential to be oppressive. Kress's definition of colonisation is oppressive to the extent that it makes invisible the lived experience of the soldiers and the people being colonised. Again, feminist poststructuralist theory is more interested in definitions that encompass both the political power and coercion *and* the lived experience of it, both from the position of those coercing and those coerced. The combat version of colonisation makes it visible or analysable primarily from the point of view of the powerful. This way of conceptualising talk has interesting parallels with the 'agonistic' model of debate defined by many scholars (particularly in the Oxbridge tradition) as the only way in which debate or even conversation can take place. In this model the conversants are combatants each trying to demolish the other's position and to erect[6] their own in its place (Ong 1982). The powerful teacher, like the coloniser, sets up an illusion of a genuine debate but with no doubt in his mind that his version is correct, that his version will demolish and obliterate the version of the student.

But there is another kind of conversation in which each listens to the other, not to find the weak points through which it can be entered and dismantled, but to comprehend what is said from the point of view of the speaker and to see whether one's own understanding can be elaborated, made richer, expanded in light of the new way of seeing made possible by listening to the other. 'Do you mean. . . ', 'Is that the same as', 'That sounds like the time I. . .' are the kinds of opening responses used in such conversations. These have the function of facilitating the speaker's telling through the weaving of connecting threads between the meanings available to one with the meanings being expressed by the other. One kind of conversation is a violence, the other an opening up of possibilities—at least ideally. In listening to others in this way, one multiplies the possible ways in which the world can be seen and experienced, one achieves through such conversation, the possibility of multiple 'I's' who can know and talk about the world from more than the one position of a single ego locked into a unitary interpretation of the world.

A most vivid example of this different kind of power was given to me when I was teaching a course on gender and schooling to students in the USA. One of the students came to me in a state of extreme distress telling me she would have to withdraw from the course as she was unable to write anything. The events in her life had overwhelmed her. She had no sense of control over what was happening and seriously doubted her own sanity. She told me that her lover, the man she was engaged to marry, had sexually molested her daughter and that she had been forced by the legal structures to report him or risk losing her daughter. She had thus destroyed her family unit and was now being forced to submit her daughter to forms of activity that seemed unquestionably destructive. Her sense of failure as a partner and as a mother were overwhelming. Her attempts to deal with the situation were directed at herself—at both searching for, and blaming herself for not being able to find an acceptable way of dealing with each aspect of the crisis. I suggested that she look at each of the discourses that she was caught up in and see how each one made some things sayable and do-able and precluded others. I suggested if she could locate which discourse was being used and how it constituted her in each of the contexts in which she was caught up, she could stop torturing herself about the fact that she could not find a consistent moral position from which to act. I also suggested she look at where the power rested in each discourse, in particular looking to see which of them as an individual she could successfully refuse and which ones she was

---

[6] Note the male metaphor here, deliberately chosen because I associate the agonistic model with male forms of conversation (cf Tannen 1990).

for the moment powerless to refuse. I named each of the discourses that I thought she had made relevant in the telling of her story and gave her examples from her own chaotic outpourings that illustrated each discourse. Over the next few days she wrote an essay called 'Poststructuralism as a map through a crisis'. Once she had written this she no longer experienced herself as being in crisis. She no longer saw herself as morally flawed, since her perceived 'flaw' had been not to achieve herself as coherent in the way the humanist/modernist versions of personhood convince us that we should be. Once she had seen the constructedness of such a model of the person, she no longer felt morally obliged to achieve it. She could see that the central protagonists in some of the discourses she was caught up in had power to assert their discourse as the only one that would be made relevant and inside of which she could only do as she was told. Having seen this, she was able to act coherently and constructively within the constraints that were now visible to her, to protect her child as far as she was able, to deal constructively with each of the players involved, and not to scatter her energy blaming herself for not being able to assert the dominance of the discourses through which she understood events, nor to find coherence amongst them. What she wrote is as follows:

POSTSTRUCTURALISM AS A MAP THROUGH A CRISIS

INTRODUCTION

I had two problems; I was enrolled in a class requiring a poststructuralist analysis and I had a personal tragedy in my family. Fortunately, the obsessive thought clusters surrounding the crisis lend themselves to an illumination of Chris Weedon's position that:

'Discourses are more than ways of thinking and producing meaning. They constitute the "nature" of the body, unconscious and conscious mind of the subjects which they seek to govern. Neither the body nor the thoughts and feelings have meaning outside their discursive articulation, but the ways in which discourse constitutes the minds and bodies of individuals is always part of a wider network of power relations, often with institutional bases'.

Certain questions have primacy: What has happened? How and why has it happened? What must I do? But the answers that arise cannot be separated from the various discursive frameworks from which they are supplied—which do not necessarily support each other. These contradictions which undergird my thoughts and actions create confusions. These confusions underscore the possibility that I not be unitary but rather essentially a conglomeration of fragments. Given this piece-by-piece aspect of my being—my only hope for empowerment lies not in accepting only the few pieces which seem to jibe but rather in sorting out as much of the mess as I can. I cannot separate myself from the power bases in my society—but I can call out where they are and what they are doing in their construction of me and my situation. My ability to recognize discursive frameworks is my power.

WHAT HAPPENED

A man, whom I will call Josh, had a single session of manual oral genital contact with a five year old girl, whom I will call Vera. He also showed her how to masturbate him and ejaculated in front of her. At the time Josh was

28

engaged to marry me and the child was and is my daughter. I heard about the incident from Vera the morning following the evening when it happened.

THE ORGANISATION OF THE ANALYSIS

When presented with a rough chronology of events following and including Vera's disclosure, Bronwyn Davies suggested that I sort out the various intersecting frameworks in operation. By her formulation there are at least five discourses in action if I give each angle a key word I'd call them: legality, brotherhood, childhood, sexuality, and psychology. And finally I add one more—the perspective of the trance channel.

LEGAL/CHILD ABUSE/MORAL RESPONSIBILITY/PUNISHMENT

Under New York State Law, oral genital contact between adults and children under the age of eighteen is a crime. Members of certain professional categories which regularly deal with children (teachers, pediatricians etc.) are mandated to report suspected cases to a telephone hotline in Albany, the state capital. These cases are referred to local departments of social services which must, by law, complete a file on the situation in sixty days. These files are then filed in Albany. The investigation has law enforcement aspects and social work aspects.

On the Monday following the Friday disclosure I was told by one of Vera'a teachers that she was uncomfortable with both the knowledge of the incident and the knowledge that I hadn't called the Hotline. She advised me to call for my own protection so as not to appear suspect when someone else made the call. She also said that I should take the child to a doctor to cover myself legally should questions arise about my protection of the child.

Tied in with this were ideas of Josh as being a dangerous, unstable entity from whom children needed to be protected. When I called the hotline—but before I gave them the information—they said, 'How do you know that he won't do it again and perhaps with worse result?' When I told the story my subjectivity was organized around protection of the nation's children and setting the teacher's mind to rest about her legal responsibility.

The next day a local social worker called me and made an appointment at a police station for her and me, my daughter and a juvenile detective. I requested that the interview be taped and the the officer not wear a uniform.

The interview was not taped and it was obvious to the child that we were in a police station—that her and Josh's action were connected with this legal framework.

I said that I called the hotline so that the teacher wouldn't have to, but the officer replied, 'They wouldn't have taken her testimony anyway—she's not a family member.' This statement clashed with the teacher's and created anxiety for me because her fears had been instrumental in my desire to call the hotline.

The officer took very sketchy notes—all he needed to know was that the child was saying that a crime occurred. He could get the written details from my deposition. Her understandings and feelings were not his issue.

I asked what was likely to happen to Josh. The detective said, 'I am not a psychologist—I say that homosexuality and pedophilia don't go away and you've got to lock these people away.'

I wouldn't sign the deposition, asking to speak first to a psychologist and a lawyer. The social worker asked if the child had had a medical exam, when she learned that the exam had not included complete blood tests for venereal disease she said that would have to get done. The issue is legal coverage not avoiding trauma to the child.

She also said that the child's testimony would need to be videotaped at a later date. This clashes with the psychologist's assertion that Vera not be lead to talk about the incident artificially—as we will see.

I didn't like giving up control and I phoned the social worker and said that I wished that the investigation (which I had launched the day before) be stopped. She told me not to be ridiculous and warned that not cooperating fully with the police and her organization could be construed as child neglect.

I called a lawyer. He said that the child's testimony was all they needed and with or without my further consent the police had all they needed to pursue Josh and if my services were needed I could be subpoenaed in court.

My parents counselled that they regarded Josh as an animal, with no good reason to live.

When I returned to the Police Department and signed the deposition the detective said that the written work would cause the jury to go easier on Josh than my spoken testimony.

'It looks better for him if he doesn't have to face a hostile witness' he said.

'If he confesses, he'll get counselling—if he won't confess—prison.' Also, I learned that if Josh confesses, Vera won't need to be videotaped.

******

Myself as a law abiding citizen.

Within this legal framework—the interest is in getting Josh sentenced to ensure that he gets help psychologically and to protect other children. Sentencing will mark him as a convicted child molester and make him legally suspect for the duration of his life. My personal beliefs about how to help people and how to spare my daughter psychological pain are not an issue here.

CHILDHOOD/INNOCENCE/VULNERABILITY

This discursive framework involves my daughter's innate sensuality and her need for protection. A five year old has the capacity to enjoy physical intimacy and novelty. She trusts adults to set limits on what is appropriate. When she spelled out what happened, with each successive step she said, 'And I thought it was okay—because it was Josh and he was in our family'. After Josh ejaculated, Vera recognized the physical manifestation of sperm as being what Mommy told her joins an egg and makes a baby—so that was okay.

When Josh said, 'Vera, we must never do this again and you must promise not to tell Mommy,' Vera began to have doubts.

Interestingly, when Josh describes his participation he says, 'My personality completely disintegrated and I became a pleasure loving child who just wanted to have and create good feelings with no capacity to think of consequences.' His interpretation is that to do these actions he joined her in childhood rather than wrenching her up to join him in adulthood.

******

My self as a mother who can understand the nature of what it is to be a child.

Within this discursive framework of childhood and vulnerability, as an adult I feel a sorrow that I did not protect both Josh (as an overgrown child) and Vera from this sexual contact. If I had stayed home that night my presence would have prevented it.

I imagine if I could have leaped into childhood myself (as Josh perhaps did) I might hear Vera's description and say 'that was yucky' or 'that was nice', and not tell anyone or take it farther than that. If that had been my course neither she nor he would confront the societal taboo against incest and the activity would likely continue and escalate. This imagined choice was a null choice because I am entrenched in adult realities with all the anguish of responsibility.

The evening that I learned the news a friend said that my anger and sadness was more injurious to the child than Josh's actions. But to mask or not have those feelings would be to divorce myself from all the adult discourses operating.

SEXUALITY/PLEASURE/MARRIAGE/TRUST/COMMITMENT/LOVE

This discourse hinges on the agreements that create family life—two adults will love each other and make commitments to be sexually faithful and to honorably perform their responsibilities as parents. The sexual pleasures that they share will be exclusive of others. And the physical pleasures allowed children will be monitored and restricted, that is, certain sexual lines will not be crossed with children.

The trust I had in Josh had its roots in two years of steady daily life. Previous to that both of us had been erratic and had not been able to commit ourselves to each other, or to other people so we were explicit in deepening our trust in each other.

For me the concept of family embraces parenting and spousehood. Josh, on the phone from New Hampshire, said recently that perhaps if we had been married and the bond had been greater—that when he did this thing I might not have kicked him out but rather allowed him to stay. But I can't separate husband from good father. A bad father negated his husbandhood in my eyes.

******

31

Myself as wife and mother.

This discourse is among the most painful for me because both Josh and I were seemingly in our element as family members. Just simple chores of doing dishes and shepherding the daughter to bed and then going to bed were sanctified by our commitment and love as the rituals of being in family. And that bond between Josh and me was violated by his choice to secretly include Vera in activities that were exclusively my domain.

BROTHERHOOD/CARE/PROTECTION/LEGAL RESPONSIBILITY

This discursive framework is related to the legal one with which I began but the impetus has to do with what one does to be a righteous person rather than a law abiding one.

This guides actions having to do with taking care of people—not worrying teachers, sending Josh support that gives him the strength not to kill himself, reassuring my parents that I am not cracking up, boxing Josh's possessions without damaging them.

******

Myself as a righteous person.

This is about supporting people emotionally and taking care of business. I cover all of Vera's vulnerabilities—psychological, medical, social, academic and legal—from this position (along with others).

PSYCHOLOGICAL/SICKNESS/DISTURBANCE/NORMALITY

On the phone, one day, I said to Josh, 'I don't consider you to be evil—just morally weak.'

'No, I'm not morally weak—I'm seriously mentally ill' he said.

To be evil would imply that he didn't know right from wrong, whereas to be morally weak implies a knowledge of right from wrong coupled with an inability to remain righteous. But to be mentally ill suggests that he had not the capacity to make the good choice through medical/psychological weakness rather than moral.

Josh said that his present New Hampshire psychologist, whom he had been going to prior to coming to New York to live with Vera and me, said that he had not been ready to take on the responsibility of family life when he chose to join me.

From the age of roughly 13–23 Josh was involved homosexually with a man fifty years his senior, from 24–27 he was married but he remained promiscuous, from 28–30 he lived with me., Only for a few months after separating with his wife did Josh live alone and get a sense of who he was outside of relationship. Before his selfhood was solidified, I enticed him, unable as he was to make good decisions, to move in with me.

Josh's psychologist—through Josh's description of me alone—has suggested that I enter long-term, in depth therapy.

This is the framework that says Josh needs therapy rather than prison and

32

that I need to cover Vera's and my psychology as well. This framework is at odds with the impersonality of the legal framework.

My psychologist said that Vera should be discouraged from dwelling on the incident and that I should limit talk in front of her—this flies in the face of telling the policemen and then also making a video taped testimony.

My psychologist is also leery of the proposed VD blood test on the child.

******

Myself as psychological case and member of a family of psychological cases.

This framework suggests that we are fragile and all need help.

PSYCHIC/TRANCE CHANNELING

This framework has for its perspective that of lifetimes of karma and responsibility.

The channelled entity's position was that Vera as an adult disincarnate entity—before she came into body—arranged to have this situation come about because she had the karma for it and wanted to get it out of the way before she grew up so that she wouldn't have a bigger sexual mess to go through as an adult.

Josh is dealing with the conflicts of having had polarized lifetimes as either a brutal rapist/warrior or a placid monk. In this lifetime he is attempting to reconcile these sides of himself.

My job was to redraw the boundaries in Josh and Vera's lives which I did—keeping me on course with the work that I decided to do when I came into body.

At this point I am riding the storms of emotion quite well but Josh is afraid the thunder and lighting might kill him [suicide]. My love for Josh has fashioned him, if not a stallion, a pony to carry him through the storm.

******

Myself as God/Goddess/All that is—currently residing in a body.

This framework conflicts with the psychological one—it was not the stress in the household that sent a fragile Josh over the edge but rather this grappling with aspects of heaven and earth. My contribution has been one that makes the angels proud.

WHERE DO VERA AND JOSH RESIDE

From Josh's point of view—this mammoth tragedy is a function of mental illness, largely. At this point a recognition of his responsibility for causing pain sends him into a suicidal depression. The legal ramifications are a terrifying tragedy. He has all the sides that I have of parent, citizen and spouse and each of these parts is in agony.

From Vera's present point of view—Josh has gone away to get better and he is getting better because he needs to not do sex stuff with kids.

33

Mommy is angry, sad and exhausted and doesn't read stories for a long time or with as much feeling as Josh used to.

It was right to tell Mommy but it has been awful ever since.

So?

So, I can see from my pulling out the discursive frameworks why I feel so crazy and that I'm being pulled to pieces.

Each agenda has its own reasons and loyalties that don't mesh well with the others.

The 'I' that navigates through the vegetable soup, if you will, is composed of carrot, celery and beet herself.

What the author of this story achieved was a recognition and acceptance of her own multiple 'I's' and the discursive nature of their existence. With this came the ability to move easily between them, and to judge when she could resist and when she had little realistic choice but to comply. She could tell Josh, when he rang, that she did not want to enter into his madness discourse, and she could co-operate with the police recognising the legal mandate they had to require her compliance, and again putting to one side for the moment the discourse that said her compliance would cause psychological damage to her child.

In some sense this could be seen as a deterministic position—to succumb to the imperatives of the social structures that surround us, rather than to struggle against them. In removing the site of the problem from herself to those structures however, it is possible to see both the power of the structures and the inevitability of bowing to their pressure *and* to contemplate the ways in which those structures might be worked on to change them such that they do not in the future exert such intolerable pressures. The alternative of locating the problem within oneself opens up only the possibility of endless accommodation to those structures or to ill-informed battles with them that one is almost certainly bound to lose.[7]

The question then becomes one of how resistance can best be organised and staged through collective shifts in discourses, and through positioning oneself differently in relation to those discourses rather than how any one solitary individual can pit themselves against forces that are greater than they are. Of such struggles de Lauretis says:

... identity is not the goal but rather the point of departure of the process of self-consciousness, a process by which one begins to know that and how

---

[7] One of the friends who read this text pointed out how disturbing it was not to know the end of the story—what happened to Josh and Vera and to the student who wrote the story? After giving me the essay and telling me I could use it in any way I wished, the student no longer needed or wanted to talk further. Everything was now able to be managed. As her lecturer I respected her wish for privacy and for the conversation to be closed. Without the help of therapy of any kind, and simply with the use of poststructuralist theory, she had been able to sort out and manage what had become an overwhelming life crisis. But what happened next? Like any other reader, I have been left to wonder both at the empowerment she gained from poststructuralist theory and at the way the story continued to unfold after I had left the States.

the personal is political, that and how the subject is specifically and materially en-gendered in its social conditions and possibilities of existence...

(de Lauretis 1986, p. 9)

It is nevertheless important, she says, to maintain the tension between the personal and the political (rather than collapsing one into the other) 'precisely through the understanding of identity as multiple and even self-contradictory' (p.9).

Some poststructuralist writers

Thus far I have talked about poststructuralist theory as a reasonably coherent discourse, though pointing to the different ways some men and some feminists might position themselves within it. I have not referred very much to the major writers in the field nor shown what particular contributions they have made. By way of concluding this chapter, I would like to name a few of these writers and very briefly tie some of their ideas to the ideas that I have chosen to make relevant here.

Julia Kristeva

The most significant contribution that Kristeva made to my own thinking was in her article 'Women's time' (Kristeva 1981). In that article she argued that while the various forms of feminism that had emerged over time (liberal feminism, radical and socialist feminism and poststructuralist feminism) profoundly contradict each other, each one is still necessary (Davies 1989a, Moi 1985). The possibility that we might constructively and legitimately think and speak from multiple positions within multiple discourses, not being *identified* with or bound by one is extraordinarily liberating and empowering. Understanding the political work that each discourse makes it possible to achieve, enables each person to access a range of speaking positions, to see the contradictions as inherent in the discourses rather than in themselves. While consistency and total coherence are pleasurable and satisfying, they involve a large degree of selective perception and ignorance: we need to live with contradictory discourses because we live in a profoundly contradictory world with multiple and contradictory positions and discourses which go to make up that world. Thus we can use the liberal feminist discourse about justice and equality when we are dealing with access issues. We can use radical feminist discourse to celebrate femininity, to re-vision it in positive ways. We need to do this whenever we are dealing with the downgrading of femaleness and femininity that is an inevitable result of the binary and hierarchical construction of male and female. We can use feminist poststructuralist discourse to gain the detailed insights we need into the way the male/female dualism is created and sustained through text and talk so that we can begin the awesome task of finding other ways of speaking/writing ourselves into existence.

Others have seen Kristeva's major contribution as the break from the determinism of structuralism. The possibility of the kinds of disruptions envisaged in poststructuralism are simply not possible in the over-determined world of structuralists. As Brodribb comments, 'Structuralism is existentialism without the existent, without the freedom and anguish of subjectivity' (Brodribb 1992, p. 32). But determinism is not easy to escape from, and although Kristeva made important

35

breaks in the re-valuing of subjectivity, other aspects were left intact. On this point Fraser says:

> Kristeva's intention to break with structuralism is most clearly and succinctly announced in a brilliant 1973 paper called 'The System and the Speaking Subject.' Here she argues that, because it conceives language as a symbolic system, structuralist semiotics is necessarily incapable of understanding oppositional practice and change. To remedy these lacunae, she proposes a new approach oriented to 'signifying practices'. These she defines as norm-governed, but not necessarily all-powerfully constraining, and as situated in 'historically determined relations of production.' As a complement to this concept of signifying practices, Kristeva also proposes a new concept of the 'speaking subject.' This subject is socially and historically situated, to be sure, but is not wholly subjected to the reigning social and discursive conventions. It is a subject, rather, who is capable of innovative practice.
>
> (Fraser 1992, p. 186)

Fraser goes on to heavily criticise Kristeva, however, for not adequately escaping determinism and the influence of Lacan, for seeing only disruptions such as madness, as capable of disrupting the phallocentrism of the symbolic order. She construes disruptions such as lesbianism, for example, as psychotic. At the same time Kristeva also essentialises women in terms of maternity, making no disruption to her (maternal) vision of femininity possible outside of madness.

Hélène Cixous

Of all the feminist poststructuralist writers, Cixous is the most influential in my own thinking and writing. Her major contributions to feminist poststructuralist theory lie in her ideas of writing the feminine and writing beyond the male/female dualism. Her major interest is in studying literary texts and in finding the ways in which the familiar can be disrupted and moved beyond, in writing from multiple positions, generating multiple 'I's', coming to know in multiple ways such that the simplistic division into male and female no longer makes sense. She writes about the body and the importance of writing from the body rather than from the phallocentric abstractions through which we have been taught to be/think/write. She sees as central to the disruption of the male/female dualism the disruption both of the illusion and the limitations of the rational, unitary humanist self.

Cixous invites us as readers and writers to unbind the constraints through which we have been constituted, and in particular to give free reign to the unconscious in our interactions with text. We need to see, she says, the negative effects of logocentrism, of specific forms of social structure including our own consciousness:

> Logocentrism and idealism, theology, all supports of society, the structure of political and of subjective economy, the pillars of property. The repressive machine has always had the same complicities, homogenizing reason, reductive, unifying which has always allied itself with the master, the unified subject, stable, socializable.
>
> (Cixous in Conley 1991, p. 19)

According to Conley, in Cixous's vision:

> The imaginary must be freed through the invention of other 'I's'. The socialization of the subject, its insertion into the social machine, can be obtained only at the expense of controlling the production of the imaginary and the unconscious. These pose threats to the established order that wants to relegate the Ego to its civil place. 'Character' and I.D. card go together in this restricting process ...
>
> [Cixous] urges for figuration, not characterization, with possibilities of reading in different directions. The new 'subject', which as true subject of the unconscious is always on the run, explodes codes and social orders, undoes censorships and repression. It frees, gives birth to writer and reader, breaks the contract, displaces debt and recognition. The author's signature is always multiple.
>
> (Conley 1991, p. 26)

In reading and in writing we need to break up the strictures of the unitary subject and allow ourselves to be populated by multiple egos or selves. This is Cixous's major strategy for disrupting the oppressive weight of established reality—what she calls the *déjà là* :

> To break up character and unity, linked to a linear conception of time, is a political gesture necessary to bring about social change ... [Cixous] ... proposes a fiction which by its very definition tears itself away from the *déjà là* and through its 'indomitable desire' produces a surplus reality, an excess produced by a subjectivity that has been populated by a mass of egos.
>
> (Conley 1991, p. 25)

That mass of egos will be both masculine and feminine, both and neither, allowing us to know the other, dissolving the meaningful difference between one and the other. Cixous allows the characters she creates to materialise in her imagination across and confounding gender boundaries. She says:

> I let things be done to me by whoever materializes me until one can no longer distinguish masculine from feminine. To the letter, here He is she. She is he. He or she is the marrow and the blood of the beauty (of hers, of his). There are ravishing moments when we no longer know which one of us is the mother, which one is God.
>
> (Cixous in Conley 1991, p. 33)

Cixous urges us, through our own writing, to create a vision of what is possible outside the current constraints of what is taken to be real. It is with this vision, she says, that we can begin to create a different set of realities:

> 'Write yourself,' is Cixous's call ... This call is carried out in the fictional texts ... where the endeavour is double: to re-traverse all the loci where women had been excluded (fiction, myth, psychoanalysis, and others) and to produce a subversive fiction that is not a representation of a real but a phantasmatic writing undoing censorship and repression, toward and from woman.
>
> (Conley 1991, p. 52)

Cixous's programme is to undo the boundaries between fiction and reality, the conscious and the unconscious, male and female. Her interest is in unleashing the creative energy that can come from breaking down these boundaries. In Conley's words:

> What appears as feminine and masculine today would not come back to the same. Difference would not be based on opposition but on a bouquet of differences. But we still muddle, with a few exceptions, in the old. ...
>
> Laws of society, through correct repression of drives, have divided individuals into men and women. 'Nowadays, few are those who accept the uncertain beings on the side of poetry who admit the component of the other sex.' Because for Cixous, writing from the imaginary implies the invention of 'other I's', the poet *is* more open to otherness. She follows the post-revolutionary myth of the artist as subversive and effeminate. Poetry, like other arts, questions and transforms ideology. ...This is not to say that to create, one must be homosexual, but that there is no invention without other I's, no poetry, no fiction without that of a certain homosexuality, therefore of bisexuality. ...[for Cixous] Concept and identity give way to unending metamorphoses without a stable 'I', where there is no more opposition between world and art, real and imaginary.
>
> (Conley 1991, p. 59)

Feminine subjectivity is, in Cixous's view, more creative than the masculine. She does not see what she calls the feminine economy as solely the domain of the female sex, though she does see it as something men have generally suppressed in their achievement of the masculine. Again, according to Conley:

> She distinguishes between two economies, one *masculine* ...: centralized, short, reappropriating, cutting, an alternation of attraction-repulsion; one *feminine*: continuous, overabundant, overflowing. These economies produce differences in inscription on the textual level, but they do not refer to one or the other of the sexes in exclusive fashion. They are, at all times, to be found in varying degrees in *both* men and women. Yet because of cultural repressions, an economy said to be feminine may more often be found in women.
>
> (Conley 1991, p. 98)

At the same time, because women have long been silenced, and have been heard by men as having nothing to say, a great deal of women's effort must be directed to finding ways to speak the feminine. At the same time as they tap their creative energies to multiply themselves and move beyond the male/female dualism, they must connect with their own bodies, their own unconscious, and speak what they are inside an oppressive gender order:

> ... that is what Lacan said, when he spoke of women and of their pleasures: 'They have nothing to say, they cannot speak.' Fine. That means that he cannot hear them. It means also that he does not know anything about it. He says it clearly when he says: 'All right, if you have something to say, say it.' But he thinks that women have nothing to say. That is not true. Of course, they say it otherwise. They can say it. It can be defined. I think that in the classical heterosexual scene, the woman generally obeys the masculine demand, which is to give pleasure in the masculine way, to obey the

38

masculine phantasm of feminine *jouissance*, which would be totally, exclusively genital and which leads to effects of inhibition, frigidity, in women. But a woman who is not deprived of her body must be able to find something of it again, and of course it is up to her to talk about it, to inscribe something of it; it is absolutely not organized in the centralized, ritualized way of men, that is true. But women have to say that, and their best listeners will still be women. I am trying to say a little of it in my texts.

(Cixous in Conley 1991, p. 158)

Jacques Derrida

Feminist poststructuralists have an uneasy and ambivalent relation with authors such as Derrida and Foucault. Many of their ideas have been taken up with much excitement and used productively (Diamond & Quinby 1988). Yet precisely because they are male and therefore have access to the privileged position of being unmarked in terms of their gender, they often presume that they write as persons and their misogyny is not visible to them. Some writers like Brodribb (1992) have argued that they have to be abandoned because of their misogyny, that it is dangerous and self-destructive to take up their ideas and hope to peel off the misogyny and not be influenced by it. Others argue that we can gain much by picking out what we want of what they have to say, but always subjecting their texts to the very critiques that they have made it possible to engage in.

Derrida's most significant contributions, as mentioned earlier in this chapter, are his ideas about deconstruction of text. Deconstruction involves finding the hidden metaphysical binarisms that underlie and structure western thought, finding a way in between the binarisms and breaking them open. Using an idea he attributes to Heidegger, he talks of putting concepts *sous rature* or under erasure. That is, while we need to go on using a concept because we have not yet found a way to make sense without it, we need to signal that the concept is a problem and needs eventually to be erased. Derrida both prints the word so it is legible and places a cross through it to signal this double approach. Both to hold something and to signal that it needs to go breaks up the usual rationalistic, linear ways of thinking in which we are all trained. According to Sarup:

> Derrida has provided a method of 'close-reading' a 'text' very similar to psychoanalytic approaches to neurotic symptoms. Deconstructive 'close-reading', having 'interrogated' the text, breaks through its defences and shows that a set of binary oppositions can be found 'inscribed' within it. In each of the pairs, private/public, masculine/feminine, same/other, rational/irrational, true/false, central/peripheral, etc., the first term is privileged. Deconstructors show that the 'privileged' term depends for its identity on its excluding the other and demonstrate that primacy really belongs to the subordinate term instead.

(Sarup 1988, p. 56)

Derrida shows how the authority of discourses is established, in particular through *creating the very realities they set out to analyse or describe* by using (a) the achieved co-incidence between the thing talked about (the signified) and the

39

representation of it (the signifier) as evidence of their veracity, combined with (b) the unquestioned existence of the thing represented as separate and more real than the text representing it (Derrida 1991c). This is one of the most fundamental binarisms that he disrupts.

He shows how texts draw their own margins, dictate their own set of relevancies and yet are always heard with the reverberations of other texts, the margins in fact being written over by other discourses, other possibilities. Yet he is also interested in how to disrupt the power of text to sustain the illusions it creates in terms that are hearable to the speaker/writers:

> The movements of deconstruction do not destroy structures from the outside. They are not possible and effective, nor can they take accurate aim, except by inhabiting those structures. Inhabiting them *in a certain way*, because one always inhabits, and all the more when one does not suspect it. Operating necessarily from the inside, borrowing all the strategic and economic resources of subversion from the old structure, borrowing them structurally, that is to say without being able to isolate their elements and atoms, the enterprise of deconstruction always in a certain way falls prey to its own work.
>
> (Derrida 1991a, p. 41)

He draws attention to the weaving of text, not as a tissue which has no spaces, but as something woven, the process of weaving being central to that which is woven, along with the spaces, the silences, that which is not there:

> What is then woven does not play the game of tight succession. Rather it plays on succession. Do not forget that to weave (*tramer, trameare*) is first to make holes, to traverse, to work one-side-and-the-other of the warp. The canal of the ear, what is called the auditory meatus, no longer closes after being struck by a simulated succession, a secondary phrase, the echo and logical articulation of a sound that has not yet been received, already an effect of that which does not take place.
>
> (Derrida 1991b, p. 168)

Another way of talking about these strategies is to talk about 'reading against the grain'. Instead of achieving the reading the author imagined or intended, reading against the grain involves disrupting that frame through a deconstructive examination of the detail. Reading with the author is like planing with the grain of the wood. The feeling is pleasurable, the wood is unified and whole and smooth, as are the curled peels of wood that are planed off. Planing against the grain, in contrast, is unpleasant, the shoulder jars, the unity of oneself with the wood is lost. The gritty, sharp, detailed, complexity of the wood stands up in disorganised spikes. It is not possible to see the wood in the same way any longer. But one's understanding of the wood is much richer and the smoothness is seen as an achieved relation with the wood rather than the essence of the wood itself.

Michel Foucault

Foucault's influence is everywhere present in poststructuralist writing. His writing makes it possible to see the processes of knowing and being quite differently. He was fascinated by the systematic ways in which discourses go through sudden shifts so making one set of things thinkable, sayable, others not. Instead of seeing knowledge as power to do things, Foucault was interested in the ways knowledge is used to control others, to set up systems of surveillance through which others can be managed, regulated, disciplined. What is also of particular interest to feminist poststructuralists is the recognition that patterns of desire, too, are regulated. The illusion of the humanist self as generating its own desires (and at the same time recognising itself through those desires) is shattered through the analysis of the means by which our patterns of desire are structured through the knowledges we are subjected to/by. Again, according to Sarup:

> Foucault's work shows how in the eighteenth century processes of training and regulation of human bodies emerged in a wide range of specific institutional locations: in factories, prisons and schools. The overall outcome of these disciplinary practices were bodies that were useful and docile, productive and subjected ...

> Foucault draws attention to the dissolution of the forms of group identity characteristic of traditional societies, and their replacement by a form of identity which depends increasingly upon the capacity of the individual to reflect upon and articulate the domain of private experience.
>
> (Sarup 1988, p. 79)

His later writing reconceptualised power so that we can begin to see its shifting, partial nature and the way it is embodied in ways of speaking and acting and in the positions allocated within discourse. Martin says:

> In an interview with J.L. Brochier, Foucault describes his focus in this way: When I think of the mechanics of power, I think of its capillary form of existence, of the extent to which power seeps into the very grain of individuals, reaches right into their bodies, permeates their gestures, their posture, what they say, how they learn to live and work with other people. According to Foucault, power comes from below; it is induced in the body and produced in every social interaction. It is not exercised negatively from the outside, though negation and repression may be one of its effects. Power in the modern world is the relation between pleasures, knowledge, and power as they are produced and disciplined. The state is not the origin, but an overall strategy and effect ...
>
> (Martin 1988, p. 6)

Foucault's particular project was to break open the illusion of objective truth by attending to the detail of how it is arrived at—by catching it in the act of the 'formation of objects, formation of the subjective positions, formation of concepts, [and the] formation of strategic choices' (Foucault 1972, p. 116). His strategy was to develop a way of thinking which might show the way in which systems of thought *create* uniformity rather than observe it. 'I am trying to show', he said, 'how a domain can be organised, without flaw, without contradiction, without internal arbitrariness, in which statements, their principle of grouping, the great historical unities that they may form, and the methods that make it possible to describe them are all brought into question' (Foucault 1972, p. 114).

Fundamental to that bringing in question was the disruption of the way in which

41

historical documents were traditionally treated as the transparent medium through which the 'real persons' or great men of history could be revealed. Instead Foucault made visible the methods that historians used to create their subjects through their interpretations of the documents they chose to privilege. Through the use of Foucault's strategies the 'subjects of history' were effectively killed off and in their place, the processes through which historians created those subjects were revealed.

Much feminist writing has succumbed to and also recoiled from the claim that burgeoned out from Foucault's killing off of the historical subjects: 'the subject is dead' had become a catchcry of many a poststructuralist. Yet at the same time Foucault's writing had opened up the possibility of theorising a subject who is simultaneously made a speaking subject through discourse and who is subjected by those discourses. It is through this latter possibility that feminist poststructuralists in particular have explored the processes of their own subjection. As I said in my paper on women's subjectivity:

> Poststructuralism offers those who have never been recognized as having the subject status that men have had a way of recognizing the means by which they have been subjected, made object, deprived of agency, and inscribed with patterns of desire that hold that oppressive cultural pattern in place. Poststructuralist discourse offers a critique of the celebration of masculinity and its equation with rationality and confirms for women their sense of self as embodied, and their emotions, desires, feelings as a legitimate part of reason. For women, poststructuralism does not offer the death of the subject but the means of claiming the right to subject status––a subject who realizes, recognizes, speaks, writes her (collective) subjected condition and searches out the ways in which the patterns that hold that subjection in place can be subverted and turned to other ends.
>
> (Davies 1992, pp. 58–9)

Foucault's strategies are not used here so much to illuminate the fictionality of the constructions of history as to locate the detail which stands outside usual systems of thought and which illuminates the creation of ourselves as the fictional subjects of our own histories, with all the intensity and passion that is entailed in being and becoming the specific subject that one is. We can look at the creation of ourselves as gendered subjects and at the creation of the gender order as 'real'—as 'objective truths' which are taken to be independent of any viewer or any person's actions, or any speaking. Attending to the detailed specificity of any discursive act opens up the possibility of disrupting the apparently 'objective fact' of two genders. It makes it possible to ask how that 'fact' is ongoingly and convincingly achieved as fact despite the extraordinary diversity of masculinities and femininities, despite the extensive overlap between the ways of being called masculine and the ways of being called feminine, and despite the manifest existence of people who happen to have male genitals but behave in a female way and vice versa.

But details of themselves cannot break the bounds of a system. It also requires a shift in perspective away from seeing language as transparent towards understanding its constitutive force—of objects and subjects, of concepts and of choices. So one looks at the detail (as we can find it) manifesting the constitution of each of these and of gendered subjects in particular. In a fundamental sense then, there never is any subject/object to be studied—only its discursive formation. The more detail we can find in relation to the multiple possible formations, the more likely we are to undo the illusion of the independently existing subject/object and to find ways of seeing how it is that subject, object and discursive practice are mutually constitutive elements of the life process. It is this shift in perspective that leads us to focus on language in our attempts to dismantle oppressive forms of gender relations.

Chapter 2
A primary school classroom and the Whitlam dream

One of the terms used by critical/sociological theorists to describe the kind of teaching that might be done in relation to gender is 'emancipatory' teaching. Emancipation means freedom from social restraint or moral inhibitions. Emancipatory teaching is the attempt to move towards that ideal state. But any new discourse, even a discourse taught in the name of liberation from particular forms of oppression, necessarily brings with it its own set of restraints and inhibitions. Any teacher who wishes to teach in emancipatory ways, whether it be in terms of gender, class or race, or all of these, is thus caught up in a number of dilemmas. Central to those dilemmas is the fundamental contradiction between, on the one hand, the power and authority, even obligation, that teachers have in the lives of their students to constitute them both explicitly and implicitly through discourse and, on the other, the belief that being thus constituted will be liberatory or emancipatory for the students. To the extent that discursive practices shape or make real certain ways of being, they are constitutive of the persons who take them up as their ways of speaking the world and themselves into existence. The question for emancipatory teachers to address is to what extent that *constitutive effect* can be reconciled with their *emancipatory intent*.

This is a dilemma only recently being confronted by researchers who are both interested in liberatory or emancipatory teaching and who have recognised the limitations of and contradictions in their practices through submitting them to a poststructuralist analysis (Lather 1991, Gore 1992). This is not to say that a poststructuralist analysis negates the possibility of liberatory teaching (or the illusion of it). Rather, it enables us to see precisely the constitutive power of all discourses and to open up the possibility of sharing that understanding with students. This can be done such that they and we, as teachers, can recognise the force of their and our own constitutive (discursive) acts. In making that constitutive force more visible, the possibility is opened up of informed resistance to its constitutive power. We can, as well, with the students, search for alternative discursive strategies for constituting the social world. Such a possibility does not seek to give the students the kind of agency brought about by replacing one discourse with another, but the agency that comes from giving the student the chance to see the constitutive force of any discourse and to invert, invent and break the bonds of existing discourses (Davies 1990b, 1991, 1992, 1993).

In the classroom analysed in this chapter the progressive or emancipatory ideals and practices of one particular teacher will be examined from a poststructuralist perspective with two parallel aims.

1 To look at the detail of classroom practice from a poststructuralist perspective and with the following questions in mind:
   • What kind of *context* are the participants creating for one another?
   • How are they *positioning* each other in that context?
       a what positions or subject positions are available?
       b How are those positions created and maintained?
   • Where does the *authority* lie? Where there is a text being used, what is the relation between teacher and textual authority?
   • How is *experience* made relevant?
   • What *binary or dualistic* thinking is evident in their discursive practices?
   • Are *gender relations* visible in the text of this classroom? What forms of *masculinity* and *femininity* are being made available here?
   • What *storylines* are being made relevant?
   • What *discourses* are mobilised:
       a in the content of the teacher's talk
       b in the teacher's choice of pedagogical and interactive practices?[1]
   • Whose *interests are being served* by each of these discourses?
2 To locate the moments in which a poststructurally-oriented teacher might vary their pedagogic practice from the way teaching is being done in this progressive classroom.

The chapter is organised, then, around the video and audio recorded interactions that took place in an Australian classroom in a small rural school during one morning in the early nineties. The particular class is made up of fourth, fifth and sixth graders. The teacher, Mr Good, is also the Principal. He is well known for his commitment to social justice issues and the progressive teaching style that he developed in the early '70s. At that time there was strong support for individual teachers who wanted to explore the possibilities of 'open plan' teaching. He retains the ideals and the discourses through which those ideals were articulated, and many of the teaching strategies that he developed at that time.[2] But he now finds himself positioned differently and in a radically changed context. The curriculum does not invite innovation. He is teaching in a conservative, rural, working-class area, where his ideas and ideals were not immediately compatible with those of the parents and students. Although he is now the Principal, one who has authority, he finds himself on occasion without the power to act as he chooses.

There is a sense in which the dilemmas Mr Good now faces, however, are simply a heightened version of dilemmas intrinsic to his earlier practice and to the practices of any teacher attempting to use progressive pedagogies. Fundamental to those

---

[1] A model provided by Baker (1991) for engaging in multiple readings of lessons, and which I have used to help me organise the complex layers of discourse in this classroom, involves reading the lesson from the following three perspectives:
• Conventional discourses about teaching procedures and objectives;
• Comprehension of culture and the logic of its organisation and possibilities;
• School-cultural knowledge and classroom authority relations.

[2] I have analysed Mr Good's teaching prior to his becoming a principal in a paper called 'Agency as a form of discursive practice. A classroom scene observed' (Davies 1990b).

dilemmas is the requirement that the teacher create the particular forms of knowing and being on the basis of which 'choices' can be made, and a sense of individual autonomy achieved. The foundational work for the creation of the choosing individual is necessarily an imposition since the values they use to make their choices are inherent in the discourses through which they and their social world have been constructed, rather than something that comes from their 'essential self' (Walkerdine & Lucey 1989). The power lies in the original discourse, not in the 'choosing' that follows after. From a Foucauldian perspective, as Macintyre points out, 'citizenship represents a condition of governmentality, a condition produced by the active regulation of subjectivities, and the individual of civil society is a product of domination rather than an autonomous individual' (Macintyre 1992, p. 9).

Positioning myself as author, in the text

Before I begin, I need to ask where am I in this story of a primary-school classroom. Why have I chosen this classroom and why do I tell the particular story about it that I do? Using the familiar terms of the discourses through which academics talk about classrooms, I can say I want to engage in a feminist poststructuralist analysis of a classroom. I want to show how gender is made relevant in this classroom, not because there is any evident sexism, but precisely because there is not. I want to look at the gendering process in its more subtle forms, at the ways in which the binary of male and female is kept intact in the world of this classroom, even when there is no direct reference to it. I want to connect this to patterns of power and powerlessness as they are played out in the classroom and in particular to patterns of authority. I want to examine the relation of the gendering process to the humanist, enlightenment tradition, and to look at this and other narratives that inform the life-world of this classroom. In doing this, I can attempt to bridge the gap between poststructuralist theory and the everyday life-world of classrooms. I can attempt to extend my understanding of what poststructuralist theory can enable us to see happening in that world.

In such an exercise, just seeing and naming the detail is difficult. Not only is poststructuralist theory not often applied to the details of everyday life, giving us examples of how it can be done, but, more generally, we (that is the we who are interested in classrooms and who practice in them) have learned to take the detail for granted; it is a given, an obviousness about the way classrooms are that does not need to be named. But it is more complicated than simply coming to see that which we have not previously needed to see. 'Seeing the detail' is not a process of finding independently existing objects or practices which can be named. Every generality, every descriptive term, every attempt to say what is there, constitutes the objects and practices being spoken about. From a poststructuralist perspective the constitutive act must become part of the picture of what is seen. The viewer must catch themselves in the act of seeing in particular ways. Through this kind of detailed, painful, introspective attention to detail, it is imagined that a different kind of viewing becomes possible—one not so bounded precisely because the viewer recognises the multiple constitutive moments out of which reality is made. Foucault, somewhat idealistically, imagines an end point to such a process in relation to history, in which all bounds are broken. Such a history, he says, would be:

> ... not a system, but the hard work of freedom; not form, but the unceasing effort of a consciousness turned upon itself, trying to grasp itself in its deepest conditions: a history that would be both an act of long, uninterrupted patience and the vivacity of a movement, which, in the end, breaks all bounds.

> (Foucault 1972, p. 13)

Any analysis of discourse or discursive practices must include information about who it is that is speaking, the site from which or out of which they speak and the positions available to them as speakers within any particular context or set of relations (Foucault 1972, pp. 51–3). In this chapter I must do that of myself and my own discourse as well as in relation to the teacher and the students in the classroom to be analysed. In looking at this classroom, then, it is important to specify the site as such, and what it is possible for this teacher and these students to say and do, given their locations in that context (not forgetting the locatedness of any classroom in the wider context of the school, the community and the education system). It is also relevant to state who I am as writer and what my viewing position is in relation to this classroom.

I have found several ways to insert myself into the texts I write by including my own stories—for example, my childhood stories in *Shards of Glass*, or some adult stories such as the Sano and Enfermada story cited in the last chapter. Yet, when I start to write about someone else, as I have here, I fall back into the old patterns of writing in which I absent myself. This is so even though the old positivist strategy of writing as 'the author' is one I have never adopted. It has always been 'I' who is speaking. But that 'I' has been one who followed certain traditions through which some credible story could be told, some semblance of 'truth' could be arrived at. It wasn't until I read Drusilla Modjeska's *Poppy* (Modjeska 1990) that I realised the extent to which I had been doing this still, despite my 'knowledge' of poststructuralist theory. In *Poppy*, the author writes a biography of her mother. She quotes extensively from her mother's diaries, yet the book is dedicated to her mother 'who never kept a diary'. In imagining her way into the experience of being her mother, Modjeska uses the diary form, imagining what her mother might have written, had she kept a diary. In doing so she makes more visible than in any other text I have read the necessary interweaving of fiction and fact that goes to make up any story that we attempt to tell of the 'real' world. It is a visibility that I sometimes found painful in the reading. Why couldn't she present a seamless fiction, allowing me to believe completely, while reading, that she had captured the 'truth' of her mother's world? Why did she keep reminding me through the use of these fictional diaries that this could only ever be the daughter's telling? At the end of the book Modjeska writes:

> When I began this book my intention was to write a biography of my mother and I expected that I would keep to the evidence. In the writing of it, however, I found myself drawn irresistably into dream, imagination and fiction. The resulting *Poppy* is a mixture of fact and fiction, biography and novel. To stick only to the facts seemed to deny the fictional paradox of truthfulness, and the life that the book was demanding.

> (Modjeska 1990, p. 317)

47

Poststructuralist theory makes it possible to explore that 'fictional paradox of truthfulness' in ways not previously possible, except perhaps through fiction itself. But it is a possibility not easily taken up, since old patterns die hard and new ways of telling are not only difficult to find, but are not always readily accepted by any reader. What I want to attempt to do first, then, is to situate myself a little more 'truthfully' in relation to the story to be told in this chapter.

In the early '80s I made a set of videotapes of Mr Good's classroom. When I first sat in Mr Good's classroom I was drawn in completely to the world he created for his students and, in particular, for his female students. Here was a man at once tender and funny, at ease in his own body, with evident authority and yet relaxed and comfortable, making easy connection with the minds and bodies of his students. I longed to be a little girl in his classroom, to feel his gaze directed at me in the way I saw him gaze at the girls he talked to in his class. He would like who I was. I would light up in his gaze. I would excel intellectually and he would see and appreciate that excellence. He would hear me when I spoke. He would *know* me. He would know my vulnerability and my strength and both of these would be acceptable.

Sitting there as an adult, imagining myself as a child, was not an intellectual exercise. I did not know then, in the way that I do now, that my desire,[3] my subjectivity, my life history were relevant to what I saw. But my emotions were vivid enough to intrude into my consciousness and to be remembered. Looking back, then, at the blissful transportation of myself in my imagination into that perfect adult-child relationship, I must also add that at the same time as I envisaged that perfect relationship, I was also bound and limited, since the power I had given him was to envisage me in his terms. Because of his authority as teacher, I was almost bound to defer to his perceptions anyway, but with the addition of wanting to be perfect in his gaze I gave power to what I perceived as his vision. While I might still find opportunities to express difference (as I sometimes did at school), this would always be with my heart in my mouth for the risk I was taking in daring to disagree. This recognition of the downside of my fantasy has been the most difficult for me to come to terms with in my analysis of my position in this classroom. The imagined positive positioning came at a price that was extraordinarily resistant to being examined. I knew, for example, that I was unreasonably upset when he disagreed with an aspect of an interview I did in the earlier years with his students—on the topic of his authority—and I also knew that I was unreasonably nervous at the prospect of showing him what I had written in this chapter. But I could make no sense of that anxiety, seeing it vaguely to do with the authority of primary-school teachers—but knowing that was an insufficient explanation. This additional insight into the extent

---

[3] I do not limit the term 'desire' to sexual desire as that is usually understood. Like Grosz, I want the term desire to refer to a broader notion of the sexual that is not simply genitally or heterosexually oriented. Grosz says:

> I would like to use a model or framework in which sexual relations are contiguous with and a part of other relations—the relations of the writer to pen and paper, the body builder to weights, the bureaucrat to files. The bedroom is no more the privileged site of sexuality than any other space, sexuality and desire are part of the intensity and passion of life itself. (Grosz 1992, p. 13)

of his power in my vision of being a child in his classroom (a vision which was relevant in the present to the extent that it informed present perceptions) made my anxiety appear entirely explicable and reasonable.

Throughout the '80s I used the early videotapes of Mr Good's classroom to show my own students how progressive teaching was done. As feminist discourse became more readily accessible to me and to my students, we began to notice details in Mr Good's performance that were troubling. The storylines he had for boys were different from the ones he had for girls. Girls were being constituted as students who could excel in all things, but their futures (made imaginable in the present and therefore also real in the present) were also as vulnerable, fragile beings, other to male heroic adventurers whose adventures, in turn, would be made more exciting by their attractive (sexual) presence. I began to see how, as that adoring little girl, I would have taken that vulnerability and potential (hetero)sexuality up as my own, as part of being the one whom Mr Good could recognise as someone of value.

And the students in my classes to whom I showed the videos were not always so admiring as I was of Mr Good's pedagogical style. Particularly when they engaged in a Marxist analysis of the videos, they saw him as unacceptably powerful in the lives of his students. His charisma, in this viewing, was such that his students might gain an illusion of freedom, but they were completely in his control, so willing did they seem to give him what he wanted. He appeared to be a benign dictator but with all his power concealed. When we engaged in a poststructuralist analysis in relation to issues of gender the students began to ask for a more recent video of Mr Good. What was highly visible within this framework, and made evident from within the kinds of current knowledges about and attitudes towards gender, would not have been visible or evident to us, or to Mr Good, when looking in terms of the discourses available to us in the early '80s. Increasingly, it seemed that we were watching a historical document, one that told us how gender was done in a progressive classroom in the early '80s before current awarenesses of gender had been established. The question marks that we had begun to raise around the constitution of gender in this classroom may have been unfair, since we would all probably have been 'guilty' in the same ways at the time the first videos were made.

In the early '90s I was able to make another video of Mr Good's classroom.[4] When I had written the first draft of this chapter I showed the draft and the more recently made videotapes of Mr Good to a PhD student who is interested in poststructuralist theory and classroom practice. This student, who identifies as gay, had been repeatedly sexually molested by one of his teachers in primary school. This was a trauma he had currently been coming to terms with. I was nevertheless surprised when he told me that he felt completely intimidated by the Mr Good that he saw. His easeful, unquestioned authority and his masculinity seemed to this student to be filled with threat. He imagined himself as a student in this class, not as one who would flourish, but as one who would be totally silenced. He read the classroom that he observed as one in which there was no acceptable place for the

---

[4] This was with the benefit of a small ARC grant which enabled me with Carolyn Baker to make a number of videos of primary and secondary school classrooms.

kind of child he imagined himself to be. Perhaps he, too, imagined Mr Good as potentially able to meet his desires. But having been molested by his actual teacher in a traumatic way, that very potential was frightening since he knew it to be one that could lead to the transgression of boundaries, the violation of prohibitions, and that could rob him of his right to speak and to claim his right not to be violated.

Each of these readings involves the transposition of the viewing adult back into childhood and to their experience of being a primary-school student. Past experiences of being a student clearly can be relevant to any interpretation of what is happening in the present. But they are obviously not the only relevancies. In the '80s, for example, there was a widespread interest in and talk about progressive or 'open' education. As someone interested in that discourse, I found it fascinating to watch a teacher who appeared to have successfully translated the ideals of that movement into practice.

As well, there was an aspect of Australian culture at that time that was relevant to any viewing, though not necessarily at any conscious level. There had been a transformation in Australian culture during the early '70s—during the time Whitlam was Prime Minister—that was deeply significant to a number of Australians, myself and Mr Good included (ABC TV 1992). A different set of storylines about what it meant to be Australian was made available. Those of us who picked up those storylines and made them our own ceased to think of Australia as an inferior member of the British Commonwealth, and began to see ourselves as a nation with a part to play on the world stage. No longer ruled in these new storylines by the British monarchy we had a new story in which we had power to shape our own culture, our own consciousness. In concert with this new storyline, relations with Asian neighbours were established as significant and we began to recognise our geographical location in the Asia–Pacific region as relevant to who we were. The shame of our past colonial attitudes to the Aboriginal people and Asian migrants was recognised and reparation begun with landrights and the establishment of anti-racist legislation. The shame was heavy but it belonged to the colonial past. It was possible, we began to tell ourselves, to create a new world in which old wrongs were undone. Further, we no longer had to be involved in wars not of our own making. Big brother America could not require the loss of Australian lives, and not even our own government could insist on this. The withdrawal of troops from Vietnam was commenced the day after Whitlam was elected and conscription was abolished shortly after. An injection of funds into the arts meant that our own cultural myths and legends and our own art and literature could be developed as part of the establishment of an Australian identity separate from our British past. These were heady times and the new storylines were extraordinarily empowering. Education was high on the agenda, and was seen as a means for enabling all children to gain access to a new world in which 'youthfulness and newness were linked with intelligence and a rationalism free from old pieties and fears' (Little 1986, p. 63). Rationality and idealism combined to form a powerful new vision of what each of us might strive to be and might strive to enable our students to be. The liberal humanist ideals of the autonomous individual were framed by an agenda for structural changes which would facilitate the expansion of each individual.

In the perception of many, these changes were a result solely of Whitlam himself. That, of course, is the way history is usually written, attributing changes to specific 'great men' rather than to the shifting pattern of discourses that made it possible for that man at that time to articulate something that others could hear. For those who have known and been impressed by Whitlam, it is quite difficult to adopt a totally Foucauldian position and to assume that anyone positioned as Whitlam was positioned at that time could have created the same vision and stirred people's imaginations and passions in the same way. At least it would have to be anyone with the same set of competencies, able to expand into the subject position of Labour Prime Minister and to manifest him/herself as someone of stature. Of course Whitlam could not be the *source* of these new storylines, since similar changes were happening throughout the world. But for many he *signified* the changes that were taking place. He was seen as a visionary, and as someone who changed the course of Australian history. The stories we now tell about ourselves and what it means to be an Australian are often stories in which Whitlam plays a significant part. In the minds of many, Whitlam thus stands for the changes of the early '70s. As Little says:

> Whitlam exemplified freedom to be oneself ... and a commitment to expansiveness—in lives, in the nation—which exactly fitted the hopes of both the rationalist and the romantic who in their different ways wanted above all room to move. The artists, entertainers, and commune-dwellers, no less than Fabian society members, could see in Whitlam a man whose pleasure seemed to lie in flinging open long-closed doors.

> (Little 1986, pp. 68–9)

A significant part of the change taking place was an emphasis on the capacity of each individual to take control of their own lives. 'Each individual' in this case specifically included women. The storylines for women were to be quite consciously re-negotiated first by discovering the ways they were trapped in the old ones:

> The Whitlam Government made it clear to all women—rural, migrant, Aboriginal, women of all ages, levels of education and socio-economic class—that it was possible to take their lives into their own hands and change them...

> No arbitrary and distorting assumptions were to be made about women's proper place, whether in the home or in the workplace. Rather, the preconditions were to be established for all women to take whatever places they themselves freely chose. For the choice to be truly free, women had to be conscious of how society's expectations had shaped, if not determined, their choices in the past. To achieve this consciousness, the nature and extent of sexism in our society first had to be understood, then changed.

> (Reid 1986, pp. 145, 147)

As Reid goes on to say in her paper, however, the precise detail of how these ideals, these new storylines were to be put into practice were far more difficult than she at first realised. As Whitlam's adviser on women, she found that journalists and

51

the media twisted and distorted her words and made them seem foolish. The lofty ideals ran aground over and over again precisely because new storylines do not instantly replace the old—they live alongside them, they inhabit and are inhabited by contradictory discourses, contradictory patterns of desire.[5] And any disruption to old relations of power must necessarily involve attempts to speak and respeak both the old and the new, each with their multiple fractures, their multiple contradictions.

In viewing Mr Good's classroom, then, I see him attempting to bring many of the storylines of this new vision, along with the possibilities they open up, to his students. Viewing it this way, I feel completely comfortable and at ease with what I see. But for me, obviously, the most central and significant aspect of the Whitlam vision was its attention to gender and the new storylines made available to women. This does not appear to be so central to Mr Good in his taking up of that vision, but rather is included as one aspect of a more general commitment to equity and justice for all students as that is understood in progressive pedagogical discourse.

There are thus many possible readings of Mr Good's classroom. It is important to emphasise that on the one hand these multiple possible readings of Mr Good are all constitutive readings and on the other, that no readings can be anything other than constitutive. Each viewer necessarily brings their own life history, that is their history of being positioned in the world in certain ways, of learning what to desire, what to value and what to fear, to any reading. They bring with all of this specific baggage a 'loading' which they use in the interpretation of every word, every statement. The transcribed words of Mr Good's classroom may appear as relatively stable markings on the page, but the work they are seen to do in being read are probably infinitely variable. On any particular occasion of encountering those words or statements they may be interpreted differently depending on the context (and the interpretation of that context), the reason for reading, the words that stand on the page before and after the statement, the particular moment in the reader's life history in which the statement is read, and so on. The discursive frame in particular, in terms of which the statement is interpreted, is of paramount importance. Some, or even all of the readings of his practice Mr Good might find a violence, a travesty, a threatening misreading of who he takes himself to be—of what he takes himself to be doing. But he, no more than I, can provide the definitive and final reading of the statements that occurred on that morning in his classroom. In reading his own statements he cannot recreate precisely the moment of their utterance, and even should he be able to do so, he could not provide an exhaustive account of all that was being made relevant for him and the students in that particular moment. What he can

---

[5] This multiple layering is like palimpsest. This is a term to describe the way in which new writings on a parchment were written over or around old writings that were not fully erased. One writing interrupts the other, momentarily overriding, intermingling with the other; the old writing influences the interpretation of the imposed new writing and the new influences the interpretation of the old. But both still stand, albeit partially erased and interrupted. New discourses do not simply replace the old as on a clean sheet. They generally interrupt each other, though they may also exist in parallel, remaining separate, undermining each other perhaps, but in an unexamined way.

bring to my readings is a detailed insider's knowledge which may shift some of my interpretations if they lead me to believe that my interpretations are based on flawed assumptions, mis-reading or inadequate information about the participants or the context. Perhaps of more interest is the possibility of bringing to the transcribed statements on the page another dimension, another way of reading what is there, a reading that comes from him as participant with a particular investment in the interpretations that are made of his identity.[6]

Mr Good's positioning of himself in the text of his classroom at the time the video was made

When Mr Good first moved to the position of principal, he experienced a number of dilemmas. One was related to his ideals and to what was possible or practicable in this setting where the parents, unlike in his previous position, had not chosen him for their children because of his progressive style of teaching. Another was related to his idea of himself and his history in the everyday world as one who is on the side of the powerless compared to his present position as one who is deemed to have authority and must on occasion use that authority in ways that he may not feel at all comfortable about:

> Helen[7]   Right, OK ( ) sort of ideas of authority and control, that sort of thing, if, where do you see yourself in the idea of the issue of authority and discipline and those sort of things?

> Mr Good   Again, depends upon the situation because my role changes throughout the day, at times you need to be a figure of authority, other times you need to be a friend, other times you need to be a counsellor, other times you're just an ogre, you've got to be

The position of principal does not give him the power to dictate what will be taught to the students in his school—rather it gives him access to another forum in which he can argue for the kind of curriculum he would like. As principal he may even have less power to innovate than he did as a (subversive) teacher in a different context and a different time:

> Mr Good   Yeah, you know I commenced teaching in a very very exciting time. It was just after Whitlam had been elected and it was *really* exciting and you were given freedom to innovate and those, you know those times don't exist now. The sorts of, you know the curriculum that's coming is good curriculum there is no doubt about that but by the same token the opportunities for alterna- tives within a system just don't exist, there's a stereotype that's going through... Yeah well I am, you know, I am not conserva- tive by philosophy. But it's the system that is forcing conserva-

---

[6] As it turned out, when Mr Good read this chapter he did not want me to change any of it.

[7] The research assistant on this project was Helen Stasinowsky. She was responsible for video- and audio-taping a number of classrooms and then in consultation with Carolyn Baker and me, carrying out a set of followup interviews with each of the teachers.

tism on people. For example I went to my first principal's
conference and I went in there and I had a look at it, and I looked
around and I thought ... well I've made it. Now I was physically
ill that evening because I thought my god this is what you got
yourself into. I'm one of them. Right, so there's that sort of
feeling, but that was five, six years ago but now you know I sort
of find that you know there are lots of great principals there that
have similar views to my own and they are fighting

Like the students in this rural classroom, Mr Good came from a working-class
background. In part because of that background and also because of his investment
of himself in the Whitlam vision, he has a particular commitment to opening up to
all students the possibilities that education can provide. His talk about what he does
is in terms of such opening up of possibilities and is about attention to the individual
child who must become a motivated learner, if they are to take up those possibilities
and 'go further' with their education. This involves the provision of 'different social
experiences' that they would not otherwise have, and a shift away from placing
himself in the position of one who has the answers, to one in which the students are
able to position themselves as active, 'motivated' learners. His talk can be read both
as straightforward liberal humanism, or belief in individuals and their rights, and
also in terms of the Whitlam ideal of the 'freedom to be oneself' (Little 1986, p. 68),
freed from 'distorting assumptions', with students taking 'their lives into their own
hands and chang[ing] them' (Reid 1986, pp. 147, 145):

Helen   Where (do) they hope to go when they sort of finish school and
          that sort of thing, they have/

Mr Good   Um they'd be back working on properties, truck drivers, some
          of them will probably aspire a little higher, yes. Generally that's
          about the level, some of them have higher aspirations... You've
          got to, you know you look, at the needs of every individual child
          and you've got to shape your curriculum and whatever other
          tools you have to [meet the needs of the child]... Um, the
          challenge is to broaden their horizons. So there's a fairly heavy
          emphasis on exposing them to different social experiences and
          providing experiences that they probably wouldn't have ... The
          individual is very important, that's just a philosophy I've sub-
          scribed to that the intrinsically motivated child is going to go
          further than the child that needs you to juggle chalk every time,
          so that's very very important. So the approach or the whole
          approach is geared to bringing out that sort of intrinsic nature of
          motivation in the child

When asked about the specific limitations that girls experience through having
to wear the uniform dress, he explains that he is not pro-uniform for anyone, but the
parents are. He does not pick up on and elaborate any philosophy specifically to do
with gender, claiming that girls, like anyone else, can flourish in his classroom.

Helen	Ah the girls, what is the uniform here, do girls wear their dresses and/
Mr Good	Yes, yes there is a uniform, I'm not pro-uniform and I've tested the water there, no one/
Helen	So parents, I was just talking to another school this morning and they're finding a battle too, a very traditional sort of school and where they're trying to encourage, for girl's uniforms particularly, that was the most controversial, boy's uniforms were fine, but to try and introduce a range of, so that the girls could wear you know trousers or tracksuit or something if they wanted to but the parents there are very resistant to that. What sort of a feeling here, or are your parents/
Mr Good	Well I think there are other issues that are far more important. So I've raised it once and it was fairly obvious that it was going to be a fairly contentious then I don't, you know I can see that there are other issues that are far more important like getting kids down into capital cities, you know they're far more important issues than uniforms
Helen	No that's interesting, ( ) on the gender things that Bronwyn's particularly interested in, are you aware of treating girls or boys any differently in your class, your response to them?
Mr Good	Not really, no. Obviously there are differences but no, not really.
Helen	You don't, your expectations for either group is, is it different in any way, perhaps where you see them heading or do you see them all as a group of students?
Helen	I just see them all as a group of students, I've just, you know I've always looked at students like, our musicians, our good musicians tend to be girls, ah, our good sportspeople tend to be boys, it's just the way it's worked out here... Where I've been before I think the good musicians have generally been girls and the good sportspeople have been girls

His position on gender appears to be that it is better not focused on specifically but encompassed within the broader progressive ideals for all students. His response to the question of whether he is aware of treating them differently is interesting: 'Not really, no. Obviously there are differences but no, not really'. The 'Not really, no' can be heard as a claim that he does not treat them inequitably. 'Obviously there are differences' makes reference to his everyday knowledge that girls and boys are culturally constituted as different. The final 'but no, not really' is to return to the initial claim that these differences are not relevant when talking about equity. In relation to the discussion in chapter 1, then, the unmarked nature of masculinity and the marked nature of femininity is left intact. The visible differences between males and females are deemed irrelevant to (made invisible in relation to) the progressive educational ideals for all students. And in terms of the Whitlam vision on gender, therefore, Mr Good would appear to assent to equality but to dissent from the claim that oppression needs to be made visible if it is to be changed. The burden of change lies instead in Mr Good's progressive strategies. Within this discursive frame the students, both male and female, will come to want for themselves the possibilities Mr Good makes available to them:

Helen   So how do you go about sort of getting the kids to work more independently?

Mr Good   Well you set them tasks, you provide them with choice, you open things up to them. So you provide them with a variety of experiences from which they can choose. Obviously there has to be some structure with kids that are a little insecure and possibly coming from backgrounds that are a bit insecure too. So there's got to be some stability that once that's established there's security there, then you can open things up and that's taken about five years here so I had to bring it out and it's different stages for different students

Helen   So then how much autonomy do these kids have would you say?

Mr Good   It depends upon the situation but they have probably more aut- or they definitely have more autonomy than those kids in a more traditional school

Despite the constraints that Mr Good experiences and which he locates as coming from the community as well as the education system, he sees himself as giving his students more autonomy than students have in traditional schools. While noting these limitations on his practice, Mr Good has nevertheless maintained his progressive ideals. His desire is to move towards them in his practices wherever the context and his positioning and the power relations in which he is caught up make this possible.

The classroom
On the particular morning when the new set of video recordings were made, there are two major themes to the lessons. One is Australian history and the other is the Australian environment and the recording of the children's responses to it. The class format moves regularly from whole group interactions with the teacher to small group work and individual work. When the students are working individually or in small groups, Mr Good moves from one group to another and occasionally calls for the attention of the whole group to the work of a particular individual.

The day begins with informal chat and some guitar playing. The students then move into a circle around the teacher. They discuss a letter from someone they all know. This leads into a discussion about geography and then to a discussion of Iraq and the plight of the Kurds. They then break up and do small group maths exercises. Following this is a writing session. Mr Good works closely with a group of boys on a joint story they are constructing and one of the boys reads this story to the class.

They then go down to the nearby river and, again in small groups, write about what they see. Some of these stories are read to the whole group on return to the classroom. After morning recess the students come in and work on their projects of early Australian life. The teacher then gathers the students together and reads a chapter from a story about early Australian life. He then proceeds to show them how to cook rabbit stew, having dressed two of them up in clothes appropriate to the time they are studying. The extracts used in this analysis come only from the time prior to recess.

The first extract is from early morning 'circle time' when the letter is being discussed.

Extract 1 Circle Time

1 Mr Good   *(It is the beginning of the school day. Mr Good is on a low chair and the students are seated around him on the floor. Melody and Tracey, are kneeling at Mr Good's side. They have been discussing someone mentioned in a letter from Sally).* Right. Anything else?

2 Tracey   It's a man.

3 Mr Good   *(turns to look at Tracey)* It's a man

4 Melody   *(Nods)* Yes

5 Tracey   It's a man

6 Mr Good   It's a man. He's a man, even. *(Mr Good smiles in a friendly way at Tracey)* Okay. Well, that's Okay. Well, that's (that's that's O.K.) ( ) and she and she goes on to say that she's doing, Indonesian, the language. *(Melody moves away from Mr Good into the group and sits down) (Mr Good folds letter and leans forward, wrinkles brow)* Why: *(puzzled tone of voice)* do you think that she'd do Indonesian and say not um, a:h French or [

7 Tracey   [She should have done French ( ) *(Mr Good does not look at Tracey)*

8 Mr Good   German or

9 S   (She wants to do Indonesian) *(Mr Good turns to speaker)*

10 Mr Good   Right so that's that's ( ), but, but why: Indonesian? Why not sort of something that's a bit different?

11 Tracey   'Cause it's hard *(Mr Good does not look at Tracey)*

12 Mr Good   Right. But we don't do things just because *(Mr Good glances*

57

at Tracey, looks above her head then back at her) they're hard *(Mr Good smiles briefly at Tracey)*

13 Tracey   U:m

14 S(s)   What is this to do (   )

15 Mr Good   Whe:re's where's Indonesia? *(Mr Good lifts his chin and eyebrows slightly. Some inaudible words from students)*

16 (Girl)   I:n

17 S   (   )

18 Mr Good   *(Mr Good turns)* Where's Indonesia? *(acknowledges student)* Yes?

19 (Boy)   Just above us

20 Mr Good   Good good *(Mr Good gets up)* (I'll get)

21 S   Oh no

22 (Girl)   Oh Mr Good not the map *(Tracey throws herself on Mr Good's chair)*

23 Mr Good   *(Mr Good moves over to the side of the room to get a large wall map of the world.)* the map.

24 S   Oh why?

25 S   Can't we just use the globe?

26 Mr Good   (No)

27 (Girl)   (   )

28 Mr Good   (Well this this) (   ) We'll just have a look where, where Indonesia is. *(Mr Good steps through students to other side and hangs map on blackboard)*

29 S(S)   (   )

30 Tracey   Oh Mr Good I can find it , if I can find it

31 S(s)   (I can find it) (Many students call out in chorus)

32 Mr Good   All right. I'll just have your

33 S(s)	*(Students still calling out in chorus and some hands in air)*
34 Mr Good	*(Mr Good clicks fingers and raises index finger)* A:h sh sh sh *(Students immediately quiet but hands stay up and Mr Good stretches out a hand to one of the boys)* Joey *(Tracey has got up and is standing in front of the map and is looking at it)*
35 S	Sh Tracey (sit down)
36 Mr Good	Tracey sit down please *(Tracey sits down)*
37 (Boy)	I can see it
38 Mr Good	*(Joey stretches and puts finger on New Guinea. Mr Good puts his finger in the same place)* Right, we:ll not rea:lly. You've pointed- but what's he pointing to there? *(Mr Good, finger still on the map, turns to class and raises a hand indicating what he wants of them)* Hands please. Yes *(acknowledging student)*
39 (Boy)	Papua New Guinea?
40 Mr Good	Right. He's pointing to New Guinea there, but ve:ry *(Mr Good runs his finger over to Indonesia. Joey still has his finger on New Guinea)* ve:ry close
41 S	( )
42 Mr Good	That's—Indonesia is a, *(Mr Good puts his hands on Joey's shoulders and guides him to sit down)* well done. Indonesia is a group of?
43 S	islands *(some other students also make suggestions which are not audible)*
44 Mr Good	That's right, a group of islands, and it's very very close to Australia so I suppose Sally would be learning Indonesian because, Indonesia is fairly close to Australia. Indonesia's been in the news a little bit over the last couple of days. For what reason?

There are many possible readings of this extract. The most usual ways of looking at teaching are in terms of what is being taught—the content—and the processes used to establish that content. In this early morning circle time, Mr Good is using the arrival of a letter from Sally which tells them, amongst other things, that she is learning Indonesian. To help the students find a reason for Sally learning Indonesian, Mr Good raises the topic of the geographical relation between Indonesia and Australia and the location of Australia in the Asia–Pacific region. In order to do this he has to establish that the students know where Indonesia is. In the process of doing so, classroom authority relations become central to the talk. Fair turn-taking and the need for group cohesion rather than many individual voices are re-established so that the location of Indonesia can be established. The situational content of the lesson is thus that the teacher and the students will work together to achieve specific knowledges. In doing so they must attend to group cohesion ('A:h sh sh sh' 34) and to turn-taking ('Sh Tracey sit down' 35). Co-operation with the teacher in finding the answers (following correct turn-taking procedure) is established as virtuous even when one does not know the right answer. Despite Joey's lack of knowledge the finding of Indonesia is constructed as a successful joint activity ('ve:ry close, well done' 40, 42). The balancing of individual rights to speak and group cohesion is thus understood and managed by all of them except perhaps by Tracey. The naming of Indonesia as a 'group of islands' is similarly a joint production (43). The geographical political content is thus the closeness of Indonesia to Australia and to its being a group of islands, while the school-cultural knowledge content is about how students and the teacher collaborate to produce such knowledges.

Another, less readily visible content of the discussion is that people's actions are *reasonable*. This is how people are interpreted in our culture. Sally must be learning Indonesian for a reason which is discoverable from an examination of the material world (rather than her desires 9, or her whims 11). Mr Good's conclusion after studying the map is, 'I suppose Sally would be learning Indonesian because, Indonesia is fairly close to Australia'. That we should, as reasonable people, study languages which are spoken in countries close to our region is an integral part of the Asia–Pacific discourse. The students have thus been given access to the following logic:
- people act on the basis of reason
- reasonable people would want to study the languages of their region
- therefore geographical proximity is relevant to any reasonable person's decision to learn a particular language.

The students have thus been given access to the Asia–Pacific discourse as part of the process of making sense of what Sally is doing. They have learned the relevant words along with geographical information in order to be able to make sense of the Asia–Pacific discourse. They have experienced the forms of reasoning made appropriate within that discourse.

This is compatible with the Whitlam vision both in terms of its location of Australia in the Asia–Pacific and in terms of the Fabian belief in the centrality of reason. It is also compatible with humanist discourses that make reason the most central and important feature of personhood. Sally is a reasonable being and her choice comes from that reasonableness which is essential to her membership of the world in which all credible, respect-worthy people are reasonable. A form of reasoning available to the students in this interaction could be:
- reason is fundamental to being a (recognisable/acceptable) person
- I must and can achieve reasonableness
- as a reasonable person I would choose to learn an Asian language.
- my desire to be a reasonable person coincides with my desire to learn an Asian language.

In parallel with this interaction Mr Good is also visibly engaging in quite complex interactional work with Tracey. When asked later about Tracey, Mr Good says he balances giving her the attention he believes she needs and at the same time attempts not to give her so much attention that the others in the class will feel excluded:

Helen   (Tracey) comes up all the time and sort of, I thought you handled things very well actually, how do you feel about that situation, is that a normal, is she constantly sort of vying for attention?

Mr Good   Yes, she needs attention all the time

Helen   Right, and how do you feel about that sort of?

Mr Good   I give it but you don't give it to the point where the other students feel that they're being left out and they will, you know they *really* they really, they feel your mood here, they feel your, yes they feel your mood all the time, they, if I feel a bit down they're going to be flat so if I give too much to one child there are others that are going to feel left out so you've got to be fairly sensitive in the way you, especially with that little girl if you don't give enough to her then she's going to, you know she's going to have some problems, you know she really *needs* (it). And obviously it comes from a pretty, but she, you know it's fairly obvious she comes from a pretty insecure type situation, yeah

Looking, then, in detail at the transcript, when Mr Good asks for any other observations on the person mentioned in the letter (1), the two girls kneeling at his side, Tracey and Melody, draw attention to his sex/gender (2–5). Mr Good accepts this with a smile for Tracey though correcting her grammar (6). Almost immediately Melody leaves his side (6). Mr Good then raises the question of why Sally is learning Indonesian and not something like French (6). Tracey chimes in that she should have learned French (as if interpreting Mr Good to be suggesting this) (7). When Mr Good persists with the question (10) Tracey provides another answer (11). Mr Good's gaze towards Tracey is more restricted than in 6 (7, 11, 12). When Mr Good raises the question of where Indonesia is and moves to get the map, Tracey moves into his space. When he hangs the map and looks for someone to help him display where Indonesia is, Tracey positions herself in front of the map as if she had already been chosen. The class and Mr Good refuse her positioning (35, 36). Joey is then chosen and he 'helps' Mr Good to display where Indonesia is.

In her apparent eagerness to be recognised Tracey constantly positions herself in physical proximity to Mr Good. While balancing the attention he believes she needs with his management of the class as a whole, Mr Good has constantly to work to achieve the lesson as one in which everyone is potentially a contributor and in which cueing in to the answers he wants is not the way in which thinking is to be done in this classroom. Here he has the weight of usual authority relations in classrooms against him, since what the other students see Tracey doing, while evidently taking more space than she should, is nevertheless what being a student as they know it evidently entails. Thus while acknowledging Tracey's contributions he also has to signal the class that this is not necessarily the way answers are done in this classroom. Presumably to this end he ignores (7) or gives only qualified assent to her contributions (10, 12).

Tracey arguably has a lot of power in this classroom. Because of Mr Good's investment in the 'needs' discourse he must acknowledge Tracey's contributions in a positive way, however disruptive they may be of his preferred form of authority relations (cf. Walkerdine 1993). It is only by reference to the needs of the others in the group that he finds a way to justify not paying her all the attention she asks for. If I imaginatively position myself as Tracey, I read her desire as wanting to be more than just one of the students, not wanting just her fair share of time. She wants to receive Mr Good's approving gaze, but she has not yet learned to read him correctly—to know that her answers must not just involve instant cuing in to what he appears to want. She must read what he wants in a much more sophisticated way. That is, she must 'think for herself', detach herself enough from what he is saying to bring 'something of her own' to it. She must learn not to make unreasonable demands, that is, she must learn to restrain her need for attention in order to reliably get the kind of attention she wants.

In traditional schooling, authority relations were clear. The teacher had certain knowledges to which the students had to gain access. In progressive teaching, the knowledges of the teacher are de-emphasised. The students' knowledges become the starting point and the end-point. The teacher's authority along with his/her knowledge becomes problematic, even an intrusion on the lesson. The balancing act between giving students access to a new range of possibilities that they do not currently have and making it possible for them to discover these for themselves has been a constant source of tension in the progressive paradigm. Teachers have been revealed over and over again to be actually providing the answers though in a less evident kind of way than in the traditional system (e.g. Atkinson & Delamont 1976). It is difficult to escape the fact that the teacher in any classroom has knowledge that s/he wants the students to share. Someone who believes in Whitlam's vision of Australia and in all that students might be if given access to the storylines that make up the Whitlam vision, must necessarily want to work to make these available to the students.

A possibility is opened up by poststructuralist discourse for dealing with the apparent conflict between a commitment to progressive teaching and a set of values they want to pass on to students. This is to make the processes and the dilemmas visible, for the teachers and the students together to examine the processes they are caught up in and the discourses that make those dilemmas inevitable. An example of making such processes and discourses visible in an episode like the one we have just examined would be not just to give the students access to the Asia–Pacific discourse but to make visible the fact that there is such a thing. In doing so it could be pointed out that Sally has probably been exposed to that discourse and that, in taking it up as her own, she has come to see learning Indonesian as desirable. The fact that the perception of reasonableness requires an investment in the same discourses that the 'reasonable' person is using, would also be made visible. Thus, Sally's choice is constituted as reasonable only if we have access to and assent to the Asia–Pacific discourse. Mr Good shows the students how to constitute Sally as reasonable, but not how it is that this assumption of reasonableness is discursively constituted rather than intrinsic to Sally and all other acceptable people. A form of reasoning which might be made available by a teacher with access to poststructuralist discourse would be:

- reason is one powerful human competency that I can have access to
- reasonableness is understood differently within different discourses
- within the Asia–Pacific discourse it would be reasonable to study Indonesian.

This poststructuralist shift involves both students and teachers positioning themselves differently in relation to authority and to discourse. The teacher's authority can no longer rest on an assumed access to 'Truth'. Rather, teacher and students together make visible their locatedness in multiple discourses. This is not to say that they abandon themselves to an amoral relativism in which they have no investments or commitments and no passions. Rather, when they make commitments within particular discourses, they see on what basis and with what outcomes those commitments are made. Similarly, they see how others do the same within quite different discourses. They see the commonality between themselves and others constituted through similar discourses and understand the political and emotional disjunctures that arise from different discourses, different positionings and different sites or contexts. At the same time that they see the multiple positionings available to them and make choices between them, they also see the provisional nature of any of those choices: what appears correct now and what I am willing to commit myself to with passion may be able to be seen as wrong at any point in the future.

The analysis thus far has made little reference to gender. Some readers may be wondering why I have gone into the detail I have when no 'gendering' is visibly taking place. The constitution of gender does not happen independent of these other processes, so they, too, must be made visible as part of the context in which being a (gendered) person comes to be understood and played out in the current education system.

Extract 2 The Plight of the Kurds

1   (The class goes on to discuss illegal Indonesian fishing in Australian waters. This leads to a story being volunteered from Tracey about English people (poms) who caught small fish in a dam. Mr Good asks the students the historical origin of the word poms (Prisoners of Her Majesty) and asks whose ancestors were English, Scottish, Irish and European. A student then initiates a discussion about the shape of the Australian land mass and the origin of it. This is discussed in terms of evidence for the theory of shifting land masses, using the example of Antarctic Beeches that can be found in the rain forests and which they all know Mr Good is 'wrapped in'. One of the boys goes to the encyclopedia and finds a picture of the way the land masses were originally thought to have been joined. He is congratulated for his research. Mr Good returns to the news as he does each morning as part of the process of making national and world

events relevant in the lives of the students. He raises the topic of Iraq and the plight of the Kurds which was at that time receiving a great deal of media coverage. He raises the fact that the Turks are not welcoming all the Kurds and they talk about the Kurds being blocked from entry into Turkey)

2 Mr Good   Well, why are they doing that?

3 S   Oh

4 Mr Good   There's got to be a good reason. Yes *(nodding to student)*

5 S   They've got a little bridge there because (if they thought if they made it really wide or they, they just rush over)

6 Mr Good   Yes, but why why not let them come in, 'cause they're starving?

7 (Mark)   Because if they harboured the Kurds, the Iraqis might have a go at them

8 Mr Good   Good that's that's possibly one reason that that they're worried [about the Iraqis, the Iraqis attacking

9 Joey   It could start another war

10 Mr Good   Yes it could start another war. It could um, but what about a country being prepared to look after all those refugees. You know there are about, half a million, half a million refugees

11 (Boy)   That's a lot of people

12   *(Mr Good says how distressing he finds the situation of the Kurds and how sad it makes him feel, and talks about the aid being flown in to them. This discussion includes the names of the aeroplanes that are being used to fly in the aid as well as the details of what the Kurds must need to survive. Mr Good then asks them to pause and consider what they think about the situation in Iraq.)*

13 Mr Good   Who can tell me what they rea:lly think about what has happened in this part of the world over the last six months. What you really think. Just hands down for a moment. It's a very hard question, very very hard. I want you to *(pause)* real:ly *(puts closed fingers to his forehead)* think about your answer. The question is, what do you think about what's happened there in the last six months? *(pause)* Right. *(pause)* You try and tell me, *(pause)* You try and tell me *(speaking very softly). (pause)* Swailsie? *(pause)* Swailsie? What do you think about it? Yeh *(Mr Good sits down on chair)*

64

How do you feel? How do you feel about what's happened? *(pause)* That's about- how do you feel? ( ) *(acknowledges another student)*

14 S   *(pause)* I don't know

15 Mr Good   That fair. You, *(pause)* you don't know (that's cool)

16 S   *(pause)* I don't know

17 Mr Good   Right

18 S   *(pause)* There's a lot of destruction and stuff

19 S/Tracey   It's ridiculous *(Tracey laughs)*

20 Mr Good   We've got bad, its, its, there's lots of destruction, we've got, its, it's ridiculous. Why is it ridiculous?

21 (Tracey)   *(laughs)*

22 S   ( )

23 S   (It's like suicide)

24 Mr Good   It's, its, yeah. *(pause)* Can you, can you answer that? Why is it ridiculous?

25 S(s)   *(pause)* ( ) No I can't

26 Mr Good   (Okay) Right. No reason for it. I *(pause)* you know we just read about people dying and we we see it on TV but, if you can just sort of imagine *(pause)* if that happened here, *(pause)* (because) because life life is very precious isn't it? *(pause)* Hmm. Life is very precious and when we think of little Kurdish students or Kuwaiti students or Saudi Arabian students or Iraqi students *(pause)* (sort of) dying. *(pause)* That's sort of *(pause)* how do you feel about that? *(Mr Good turns head towards Tracey, apparently gets no reply and turns to front)*

27 S   *(pause)* Feels awful

28 Mr Good   *(Mr Good turns to another student)* How do you feel about that? *(Mr Good turns head towards a student)*

29 S(s)   ( ) scared, scared

30 Mr Good   ( ) *(Mr Good says another child's name and touches (her) hair)*

31 S	Distressed
32 Mr Good	It's distressing
33 S	(Distressed)
34 Mr Good	Yeh, so, do you think there's another way around having wars? *(pause)* What's a what's another [
35 Jane	( ) started the war (front)
36 S	Yeh
37 Mr Good	Is there another way than sort of shooting at each other?
38	*(The students talk about how they resolve conflicts. Mr Good congratulates two of the girls in particular for their contributions—'we all work together' and 'talking things over'. Mr Good talks about how hard it is to understand what is going on in Iraq. Even the President of America finds it hard to understand, he says. He concludes with the importance of talk in gaining that understanding)*

In discussing this extract, I want to focus on the comprehension of culture and the logic of its organisation and possibilities, with particular attention to the nature of reason as it is constructed here. As in Extract 1, the importance of reason is central to this discussion. In this extract, however, reason is linked with talk and working together as a means of attaining knowledge/understanding. As well, each individual's *emotions* are linked to this as a way of empathising or imaginatively gaining access to the point of view of others, thus indirectly giving students access to the complex relation between fact and fiction. Mr Good positions the students as people who can think/reason for themselves. He picks up their answers and tries to get them to elaborate those answers (20, 24). He places them in the same category as himself and President Bush—as ones who struggle to understand and who need to talk to come to that understanding (38).

At the beginning of this extract, in the discussion on land mass (1), the importance of evidence for interpretations of the world is established. Evidence is not presented as distant from oneself, but as including things one cares about (is 'wrapped in' such as the Antarctic Beeches). In the discussion on fishing, each child's connectedness to people of other nations is also established as is the origin of many Australians as 'prisoners of her majesty'. There is an implicit link here with the Indonesian fisherpeople who are currently prisoners. An understanding here that could be taken up by students is that in judging the Indonesians, rules of evidence and seeing the situation from their point of view will both be important.

In the ensuing discussion on the Kurds, reason is highlighted both in Mr Good's claim that there has 'got to be a good reason' for the behaviour of the Turks (2–5) and his later linking of what appears to be ridiculous (18) and fearful (28) with the absence of reason (26). At the same time, reason is not constructed as something that is done independently of emotion. How Mr Good feels (6) is made relevant and the students are invited to *think* about the situation (14–25) using their feelings and their imaginations as a possible route to making sense of the situation (26–33). In thinking of solutions to what they establish as a terrible situation, talk and understanding are strongly linked and made preferable to war (34–38). Again, the reasoning is not removed from what the students know, but related to a discussion of what they do when they have problems. Mr Good emphasises both the difficulty and the importance of the struggle for understanding.

Again, as in Extract 1, there is the following combination of elements in the discussion:
- the collaborative naming of things (poms 1, the names of aeroplanes 6)
- the use of those names to tell about the world (but added here, the difficulty of knowing what the real world is)
- the link between access to words and the capacity to reason
- the establishment of a discourse (this time pacifist discourse) as the way any reasonable person would think.

Knowledge is thus linked to history and to each child's history. It is constructed as valuable and to be struggled after, but as always uncertain. Contexts, personal emotion and knowledges are made relevant. Judgments are seen as potentially faulty even when made by powerful people with authority, such as the President of America. The value of the collective, of talk, of imagining the feelings of others is held up against the hopelessness of fighting and war. All of these are fundamental to the best of liberal humanism and difficult to distance oneself from, even knowing, from a poststructuralist perspective, that humanism is fundamental to the loss of power that comes with failing to see the constitutive power of discourse and, instead, taking up those discourses as if they derived from oneself. In viewing this from a poststructuralist perspective, I am necessarily both caught up in and trying to distance myself from humanist discourse. From this double position it is interesting to observe how the fact that the logic of the culture is not made visible as such but learned as the way any reasonable and reasoning person would proceed, leaves the humanist notion of the reasoning individual intact, that is with reasoning paramount and as intrinsic to the person rather than the specific discourse which lends it meaning. Thus the students must struggle after the particular forms of reasoning made available here, forms of reasoning that are external to them but which they must take up as their own if they are to be recognised as properly human as that is understood within this framework. There is some sense, too, in which emotion has been colonised by reason rather than legitimated in its own right. It can be seen here as a member of the binary pair, reason/emotion, and is the subordinate term. The superordinate term, reason, depends on emotion, even stems from it, but that dependency is made invisible and emotion is understood merely as a route to the superior form of knowing which encompasses all—reason. An alternative made possible through a poststructuralist framework would be to adopt a deconstructive approach. The relation between the binary pair of emotion and reason could be made visible, emotion could be valorised, played with as the ascendant term. We could try to simultaneously inhabit both reason and emotion and then neither. Finally, we

67

could look for different ways of making sense of the multiple ways we come to know—through our mind-bodies, our conscious-unconscious mind-bodies, through the traces of histories on our conscious-unconscious mind-bodies.

The major line of fault in all of this, the fissure through which the taken-for-granted world of classrooms might be called into question, is presented by Mr Good, in the idea that understanding is struggled over, even by those in authority. This opens up one potential for resistance to the beliefs of those in authority, though not to the power and centrality of reason itself nor to the discourses through which reason and power are established.

Following the discussion about the plight of the Kurds, the students divide up into groups, some going outside, to do maths exercises involving estimation and measurement. Mr Good moves from group to group, working closely with one group at a time while the other groups work independently. It is interesting to see the parallel in this maths exercise with the previous current affairs discussion. The students work in groups and talk through their tasks. They have to name objects, use whatever resources they have to estimate the weight of or distance between the named objects, and then measure with standard measurements to see if their estimates are correct. The students spend a lot of time trying to improve their methods of estimation to make them co-incide with their measurements. Value is thus placed on their own judgments, and on refining those judgments. Two boys involved in weighing objects spend a lot of time holding objects in one hand and weights in the other, teaching their bodies to know sameness and difference. During this session Mr Good calls the whole group's attention to the discovery that one of the girls made in the group he was working with. At the end of the measurement session he calls the attention of the whole group to an innovative way of estimating distance with her shoes that one of the girls working outside had thought up. Following this, the students begin work on their individual and small-group projects. One small group of boys is involved in writing about an event in their everyday lives. Again, Mr Good works closely with one group at a time. He begins working with the group of three boys. There is a large sheet of paper pinned up on the board. Mr Good positions himself as scribe at the board:

Extract 3 Danger Football

1 Mr Good	*(Mr Good has one hand resting on hip, the other leaning on the paper)* What did we do yesterday at lunchtime?
2 Boy	Played football
3 Mr Good	What sort of football did we play?
4 Boy	Ah dang- ah *(Mr Good turns to board but turns back to boys when another answer is given)*
5 Boy	Killing, killing *(Mr Good points to different boys)*
6 Boy	Danger football

7 Mr Good	*(Mr Good smiles)* Righto, we'll call it Danger Football *(writes title)*
8 Boy	No, gridiron
9 Boy	Danger football (laugh)
10 Mr Good	*(Pointing at boy)* Give me a sentence
11 Boy	( )
12 Mr Good	( ) *(Points at another boy with his hand up)* Yes
13	*(Mr Good continues as scribe for the writing of the first sentence. The talk is almost impossible to hear since the boys are all talking at once and there is much laughter. The noise from the other groups is also quite high. At the completion of the first sentence Mr Good takes the paper off the board and puts it on the floor, handing over the pen to one of the boys. He leaves the group and then returns to give further assistance. He suggests the word slope rather than hill and has them look for alternatives to the word 'fell'. He calls in question their claim that Jillian broke her arm. It is eventually agreed that she just hurt it. Mr Good then signals the class that it is time to finish what they are doing and asks Joey to read out their story to the whole class. Joey does so with encouragement and occasional help from Mr Good. He clearly feels very good about his story)*
14 Joey	Danger Football. Slippery grass and a whole lot of people playing football. Students slip over. Jillian and James were playing football. Then Jillian tripped over down the slope and hurt her arm

What appears to be happening in the construction of this story is that Mr Good is making use of the boys' displays of masculinity in football and in their cultural knowledge of football as a resource to achieve several other things related to teaching objectives and classroom authority relations as they are, ideally, from Mr Good's point of view, practised in this classroom. These include: the searching for words to best express experience (1–7, 13); the construction of sentences (10–13); the search for correctness of detail in reporting (13); collaborative work (1–14); the taking over of the task of scribe from the teacher (13). The storyline that the boys put together is of their own strength, which is illustrated by their ability to engage in dangerous activity and to survive it. This is made more visible by contrasting it with female carelessness and frailty. Although the exaggeration of the hurt that Jillian sustained is challenged, masculinist discourse is not revealed as such, not made visible. The boys could retain the impression that they had simply written a true story about the real world, not recognising the constitutive work that the details they have selected are achieving. Their enjoyment in displaying their masculinity remains invisible as such. It is unmarked. They simply enjoyed confirming the way the world is and ought to be in their telling of it.

This story that the boys wrote could be seen as an investment on their part in hegemonic masculinity, but it can also be seen as trying on one way of being amongst many others that are made available to them during this particular morning. As a feminist poststructuralist observing this exchange, though, I want more than the challenge to the exaggeration of Jillian's hurt, and more than multiple possibilities. I want the construction of (hegemonic) masculinity to be made visible such that the boys can see that what they were doing was seizing an opportunity to experience themselves as powerful and in control (fine) but at someone else's expense (a problem). At the same time it could have been a wonderful opportunity for a poststructurally-oriented teacher to point out the ways in which story is fundamental to the construction of ourselves as particular kinds of beings in the world, and the way the binary construction of masculinity and femininity is implicated in those stories.

Following the reading of *Danger Football*, Mr Good asks the students to finish off the work they are doing and to come together to talk about the next project.[8]

Extract 4 The River in Autumn

1 Mr Good	In a in a moment we're going to go down for a walk to the river. Now, I went out fishing la:st *(pause)* Saturday and I noticed so many things along the river that re:ally *(pause)* really sort of impressed me *(Joey's hand goes up)* were were just so lovely. What's happening at the moment sort of, *(Few hands go up)* yes *(To Joey who first had hand up)*
2 Joey	The leaves are falling off the trees and they go in the river and and ( )
3 Tracey	*(Mr Good points at Tracey)* Change of season
4 Mr Good	Yes that's right. It's a it's a change, a change of season. *(Mr Good asks them to name the region they live in.)* Now what season have we just come from? *(Several hands go up. Mr Good points at one)*
5 Ss	Summer, summer
6 Mr Good	What season are we going into?

---

[8] What cannot be made visible in this analysis of the *Danger Football* story is what other stories were constructed on this morning during this episode, or on any other morning. All we have is what the video camera picked up. Presumably, this story, rather than any other group's story, was filmed because this is where Mr Good was at the beginning of this session, and this group was in easy range of the camera. The point is not that the story should be taken as representative of all stories written in the classroom, but as one way in which story was done on that particular morning.

7 S   Oh

8 S   Autumn

9 Mr Good   Good. *(Points at someone else)* Spell Autumn please

10 S   a-u-t-u-m-n *(Mr Good has nodded as each letter said, and when child hesitated before 'm', Mr Good half mouths it.)*

11 Mr Good   ( ) We're just going into Autumn so there's a a really lovely *(Girl leaning on Mr Good's knees looks round then gets up and goes off camera)* sort of change and as I as I was walking along the bank there as I was walking along the bank, *(pause—Mr Good looks at girl)* is that the phone or something?

12 S   (No)

13 Mr Good   Don't worry. *(pause—girl returns and sits down away from Mr Good)* As I was walking along the bank I I saw all sorts of tremendous things, all sorts of tremendous things and, I really, I really thought of of putting down ah

14 S   The rod

15 Mr Good   The fishing rod *(pause)* and painting. And I can't I can't paint *(pause)* pretty hopeless at that but I also thought of, you know, keeping keeping a record because it was just it was was so so lovely well in a moment we're going to go take full advantage *(pause)* of that *(Joey's hand goes up, then down, then up)* and perhaps I can share with you a little bit [what I went through down at *(Mr Good extends head to Joey)*

16 Joey   [( )

17 Mr Good   Right, what do you think a a good way of sort of recording *(pause—few hands go up)* rather than [( ) *(Mr Good points)* ye

18 S   [Writing, *(Maybe Mr Good does not hear)* writing

19 Mr Good   Yes (good one)

20 Tracey   Painting

21 Mr Good   Yeh *(Mr Good points to another child)*

22 S   Memory *(Mr Good points to another child but can't hear/see response)*

23 Mr Good	We'll keep *(Mr Good taps his forehead)* all those sorts of things in mind. I'm going to take a camera down with me [
24 Tracey	*(Who has been looking at video, puts her hand up but seems to wait until Mr Good is looking at her to speak)* [Video it *(She points to video) (Students laugh)*
25 Mr Good	( ) There's the video too. I'll give you *(pause—Mr Good leans down and picks up papers from floor)* I thought it might be best if we use *(pause)* use groups we might use some *(pause)* some biggies with some littlies this time because you- your descriptive powers. *(Tracey has picked up a clipboard from behind her) (Mr Good puts hand up signalling he wants quiet)* What do you think would be a good size, a good size group when you go down there and perhaps collect a few thoughts. *(Mr Good points at boy with hand up)*
26 S	( ) four? *(Mr Good lowers his eyebrows)*
27 S(s)	Three, three, three
28 Mr Good	Yeh
29 Boy	One from each grade?
30	*(With Mr Good's help the students select groups)*
31 Mr Good	*(Talking to someone off camera)* Now you've got a good team, you've got a good team. You you two can work it out. Do you want to work by yourself? You and ( ) can work together. Okay. *(Students talk)* Now let's have your attention again please *(Mr Good clicks fingers and students 'freeze' and are silent. Mr Good is standing in middle of room with students around him)* When I walked along the river bank I sort of didn't look at a tree and say, you know 'the tree looks magnificent as the sun shines through its sort of sparkling leaves' I just looked, I saw I just, words [*(pause)* and sort of
32 Boy	[Came into your head
33 Mr Good	*(Mr Good looks at boy)* Yeh they did. Words just sort of came into my head and I sort of- words like 'sparkling' and rather lovely words. So that might be the way to go about things. *(pause)* Just look at the words that ah *(pause)* that leap into your mind when we, when we get down to the river. *(pause)* (Right) let's walk outside and explain ( ). *(They all go down to the river and write. When they return they are asked by Mr Good to read out what they have written)*

. . .

34 Mr Good	I've seen a a couple examples of what has come from the groups but um, Laurie, could we hear your's first, *(Mr Good's eyes change direction, pause)* from your group. Would you like to read it?
35 (Joey)	It's my work
36 Mr Good	*(Students talk)* It's your group *(Mr Good gestures to Joey, Laurie and Peter)* yes
37 (Laurie)	Ah, I'll read it, Mr Good
38 Mr Good	Right. Okay. Well just leave what (you're doing for a minute).
39 S	(You read my work)
40 Mr Good	*(Jane gets up, crosses room and returns with sheets of paper to sit in same place. Mr Good talks to someone at his feet)* Ah ah just wait until he ( )
41 Laurie	Dead limbs sit on [the still
42 Mr Good	[Wait a moment. Actually we might read just in a really really really loud a loud voice so we can get some ideas from it
43 Laurie	*(Kneeling at edge of group)* Dead limbs sit on the still water as the cool wind blows gently through the trees. Trout and other fish jump harmlessly through the water. Insects swim around in the calm water. Platypus bob up and down like a yo-yo looking for food. Birds sing happily in the trees
44 Mr Good	Good. *(pause)* Swailsie? *(While Swailsie gets ready, Mr Good makes comments to the previous reader)* you you sort of expanded words that sort of came to your mind into a into a piece of *(pause)* of prose Swailsie can we hear yours? *(Mr Good points pencil at Swailsie)*
45 Swailsie	*(Sitting in front of and a little way from Mr Good)* Water ripples as little trout rise to the surface of the water. Water bugs swim across the water leaving trails behind. The leaves that have fallen off trees float across the beautiful sparkling water as the sun shines on it. The trees are still as there is no wind to move them. Floating rubbish droops from the surrounding willow trees. The *(Mr Good is looking at reader but looks briefly to his right. As he looks back at reader he puts out his right hand, possibly to still someone)* sand has changed to mud under the willow trees
46 Mr Good	*(Mr Good looks away)* Wow. *(pause)* Lovely stuff.

(Two more groups of students collaboratively read their work but it is time for morning recess. Mr Good points out that they have not had a chance to hear everyone) I'll leave a big sheet *(pause)* out the front where we can each contribute *(pause)* your work. So that's your work coming from each group and we can build up a whole class's picture *(pause)* of the river that you saw this morning. *(pause)* Fair idea?

47S(s)   Yeah

48 Mr Good   Yes, yes

49 S   Yes

In discussing this extract, I want to focus on the comprehension of culture and the logic of its organisation and possibilities; in particular, my focus will be on what it means to be a writer and to be male, with some reference to conventional discourses about teaching procedures and objectives.

We have a similar pattern here as in extracts 1 and 2. The words with which to talk about the particular topic are collaboratively established (4–10). Information is gathered about the topic from the collective resources of student and teacher (2–8). In this particular extract personal experience is made the central resource and topic. The students are positioned as able, like Mr Good, to have an aesthetic experience which they struggle to express (15, 17, 31–33). They are to look for the words to express this experience not in the available discourses but from within themselves (33). Of this extract it is possible to say that the humanist version of the person is established and maintained; the Whitlam vision of Australians who are able to appreciate and give artistic voice to the appreciation of their landscape is made possible *and* progressive pedagogy is played out.

Speaking of the different school discourses about language learning, Gilbert and Taylor comment:

> Discourses like these rely on a number of key words which establish a clear dichotomy between the 'good' language classroom and the 'bad'. In the good classroom learning is natural, personal, individual, spontaneous, truthful, involved, emotional, real, whereas in the bad classroom language is associated with the unnatural, the impersonal, the premeditated, the contrived, the artificial. Holding this dichotomy together is the metaphor of 'personal voice' ... a metaphor which Derrida would argue ties the discourse to a human voice as the ultimate essence and source of meaning.

(Gilbert & Taylor 1991, p. 33)

Each student's experience of themselves as humanist subject is thus made possible through this experience of the 'good language classroom' in which they find their 'personal voice'. The students are asked to find the words within themselves as they respond to the environment. They are asked to read knowledge of the discourses through which the description of scenery is done as a personal possession, as something that comes from within, that 'leaps into the mind'.

74

Students such as Tracey can seize this opportunity to write alone, to find words and images to express the particular emotional state that she experiences. While everyone else wrote in groups, Tracey sat alone and wrote a poem which captured both the poetry of the place and her own aloneness in it:

> The River
>
> The mossy rocks stare you in the face
>
> beautiful scenery is allaround.
>
> The glittering water sparkles in the sun
>
> as weed sits lonley on the bottom
>
> of the rocky river bed.

At the same time, and from a poststructuralist perspective, there is a danger in the humanist approach. This lies in the possibility that for the subject who learns to recognise him/herself in the words that 'leap to mind', without recognising the loaded nature of the words—the political implications of finding oneself able to speak some words and not others—both the ability and the inability will be read as 'natural', as signifying who one essentially is, rather than being positioned as one who can or cannot speak in this way or that. The essentialising as one's own the words that one finds oneself able to speak, coupled with the construction of the rational consistent humanist being as the only acceptable and recognisable form of being, mean that the subject is potentially limited to the words they find themselves able to speak as the only words they can speak. A boy who feels comfortably able to produce *Danger Football* might read this as evidence of the strength and ascendancy of boys in general and of himself in particular. The poetic forms called for in the *River in Autumn* exercise might then be experienced as incompatible with this. Mr Good opens up both sets of discursive practices as ways in which (male) persons can voice their experience of the world. This potentially leads to the multiplication of 'I's' in keeping with the feminist poststructuralist project. Joey, who has successfully written the *Danger Football* story, is the first to offer up his experience of the river (1, 2) and to have his group read their story of it (36–43). It is possible to say, then, that Joey's constitution of self during this particular morning has predominantly been as writer, but also as hegemonic male whose masculinity goes unmarked. He visibly moves towards the claiming of a personhood encompassing both sides of the binary divide without recognising that his 'right' to do so rests on the way gender is constructed in our culture. In not recognising the gendered nature of his placement, he will have little with which to resist the storylines and discourses that pull him towards the male side of the binary and away from the female, except, perhaps, for the solitary example of Mr Good and the experiences of multiplicity made possible in this classroom, not least of which is the possibility of taking himself up as writer.

The autonomy and agency that Mr Good seeks to give his students—their key to participating in the Whitlam vision of what it means to be an Australian—is not necessarily something that his students can either see or desire. Yet they struggle to collaborate with him in the production of the multiple discourses he makes available to them and to imaginatively position themselves within them and, thus, to learn the

75

patterns of desire relevant to those discourses. He gives them voice, the opportunity to speak through different discourses, and for some of them, a sense of their own authority.

The shift in perspective from using the humanist concept of socialisation to using the poststructuralist concept of subjectification allows us to see the processes through which Mr Good and the students are equally caught up in structures and discourses and storylines that constitute them as who they are and who they each might be. The teacher is not, as in socialisation theory, shaping the 'internal' beings of his students. Poststructuralist theory disrupts the internal/external binary associated with socialisation theory and the passive/active binary associated with the teacher/student binary. It makes visible the ways in which teachers and students are caught up in multiple discourses, positioned in multiple ways—sometimes as speaking subjects mobilising the discourses through which they have been subjected/made subjects to powerful and liberatory ends, at other times in ways that deprive them of choice and of the possibility of acting in powerful ways.

What a progressive classroom is taken to be by each of the participants facilitates a clear set of possibilities—the sharing of discourses that make it possible for each person to actively seek knowledge and to have confidence in their ability to come to know outside the discursive confines of the world they are born into. At the same time, without access to a poststructuralist perspective, that sense of themselves, since it is discursively constituted, may slide away in the face of more powerful discourses without them ever realising just how that change took place. They may explain the change as them*selves* as having changed, 'grown up', perhaps. In contrast, a poststructuralist perspective would enable them to turn their reflective gaze on the new discourses. They could question whether those discourses have been generated to shape them for one political or economic purpose or another. They could question, as well, the assumed set of values in each discourse, and begin to locate the ways those discourses catch them up and constitute them through one limiting binary or another.

Chapter 3
Poststructuralist strategies for the classroom

The last chapter demonstrated that a significant difference between usual ideas about teaching and giving students access to poststructuralist theory as a tool is that teaching-as-usual is framed within socialisation theory. Socialisation theory posits a child whose internal being will be shaped by an education system which is external to them. The shaping is seen as inevitable and, in some sense, a competition between the different forceful shapers (peers, adults, media) who bring the child into culture and away from nature. The culture/nature dualism is fundamental to this way of making sense of the educational process, although since 'nature' has become a more valorised concept, the imposition of culture is often metaphorised, particularly within progressive pedagogical discourse, as a 'natural growth', as an emergence of the cultured/educated person out of the essential, already existent, natural being. The concept of subjectification makes much more clear the coercive power of discourses and does not try to disguise it with 'natural' metaphors.

But in understanding just how discourses achieve their constitutive force, how it is that some of us, some of the time, are constituted as powerful, agentic speaking subjects, and others are not, we can, in developing poststructuralist teaching strategies, catch ourselves in the act of subjectifying students in particular ways. In doing so, we can make that process visible to the students and develop ways to give them a speaking voice, ways that make visible the coercive power of discourse and structure and also make visible both the ways in which people are silenced and marginalised and the ways in which that silencing and marginalisation can be disrupted. At the same time, the multiple possible ways of being that become available once binary thinking is disrupted make it possible for students to see the marginalised categories in which they were previously located as providing only one of the many positionings they might take up or refuse. It is also possible for them to put the categories themselves under erasure. That is, while recognising the available discourses as currently providing an inevitable way of constituting and categorising persons, students can also see that other forms of categorisation would be less oppressive.[1]

---

[1] For example, as long as the binary heterosexual/homosexual is kept intact, then anyone experiencing sexual attraction towards a person of the same sex is at risk of constituting themselves and being constituted in terms of the latter marked and marginalised term. If sexuality is seen, instead, as multiple, fluid and complex, each person having the capacity to be attracted to both male and female, then the original binary terms have no meaning (since everyone is potentially bisexual) and, therefore, no purchase on the psyche of any individual. Specifically in relation to heterosexuality, Wittig argues:

A pedagogy informed by poststructuralist theory might begin, then, with turning its deconstructive gaze on the fundamental binarisms of pedagogy itself: teacher/ student, mind/body, adult/child, internal/external, society/individual, reality/fiction, knower/known, nature/culture, objective/subjective. Each of these underpin or hold together both what we understand as pedagogy and the discourses through which pedagogy is done. They are also some of the binarisms through which the male/female dualism is established and maintained. While they are allowed to stand as the unthinking struts of schooling, holding together, compressing, making real the authority of teachers and texts and the realities they teach, gender relations as we understand them will also be held in place. While there is not space to talk in detail about the ways in which each of these binarisms might be addressed at the levels of curriculum construction, text writing and classroom interaction, I can give examples of working differently that might serve as a starting point for the imaginations of those who want to take up the poststructuralist challenge to disrupt the gender order, both in their own lives and in the classrooms in which they teach.

In *Shards of Glass* (Davies 1993) I talk in detail about teaching primary-school children to use poststructuralist theory in their reading and writing. I show that teachers have a great deal of authority and power in their classrooms though that may be seriously constrained by their own pedagogical discourses and by the discourses through which their particular education system is currently constituted. As well, teacher authority and power is something their students constantly seize back, either through disrupting the discourses the teachers are using/asserting, or through direct resistance to teacher control. When Chas was working with the primary-school study groups she wanted to teach them poststructuralist theory to enable them to resist the imposition of gendered discourses. Like any teacher interested in giving their students some form of emancipatory discourse, she found herself caught up in the contradictions involved in asserting her authority in order to teach the students how to resist another form of authority. The girls in the St Clement's study group were perhaps the most resistive to Chas's authority. She was not a 'real' teacher. She was not one of them in that she did not speak in ways that they deemed appropriate, in class terms, for one of their teachers. Furthermore, they did not regard gender as a source of oppression. Their class position guaranteed them status which they did not see their gender undermining. They constantly refused the tasks Chas had planned for them and hijacked the lesson on to a topic of their own. They wanted Chas as a friend, someone who could give them the kind of information they wanted—not the kind of information about discourse and gender that Chas wanted to give them. The shifting patterns of power in the talk with this group are fascinating to observe. The following discussion took place when Chas had just read the students the feminist story, *Princess Smartypants* (Cole 1986):

These discourses of heterosexuality oppress us in the sense that they prevent us from speaking unless we speak in their terms. Everything which puts them in question is at once disregarded as elementary... These discourses deny us every possibility of creating our own categories. But their most ferocious action is the unrelenting tyranny that they exert upon our physical and mental selves. (Wittig 1980, p. 105)

1 Chas:	Do you remember what a discourse of resistance is?	
2 Marcella:	Oh	
3 Victoria:	Oh it's a whole lot of words, like a girl can be sexy and she's got nice hair	
4 Chas:	That's a discourse on what femininity should be	
5 Victoria:	It shouldn't, it doesn't have to be	
6 Alison:	You've got a nice bra Chas	
7 Victoria:	Can I have a look at it?	
8 Alison:	Nice and lacey	
9 Chas:	Thank you very much. So discourses/	
10 Victoria:	You shouldn't be perving at it	
11 Chas:	So what's a discourse of resistance then Alison?	
12 Alison:	It is kind of saying, oh I don't really know how to explain it	
13 Chas:	Well if the dominant discourse on what a girl should be is she should be/	
14 Tiffany:	Sexy	
15 Chas:	Sexy, she should wear/	
16 Tiffany:	Mini skirts	
17 Chas:	Mini skirts, what would a discourse of resistance be to that?	
18 Victoria:	She should shave her legs, or	
19 Marcella:	Yeah she should be posher	
20 Victoria	She should have a good figure	
21 Tiffany:	Properly groomed	
22 Chas:	That's right, they're all the dominant discourse on femininity. What would a discourse of resistance be to that? Alison what would a discourse of resistance be to femininity	

79

23 Alison:	Natural.
24 Chas:	She could have hairy legs?
25 Tiffany:	NO!
26 Alison:	She has pimples
27 Chas:	She can have pimples, she doesn't have to have a boyfriend
28 Marcella:	She can be herself
29 Chas:	She can be herself. What discourses of resistances are in this book? Now come on I want to see whether you're clever enough to be able to pull out any discourses of resistances in this book
30 Marcella:	She's not her proper self because her proper self is supposed to be a princess but in a way it sort of is her proper self because she because she wants to do what she wants to do. So if she wanted to have hairy underarms that come down to her legs she can do that

(St Clement's)

Chas had previously introduced the students to the concepts of dominant discourse and discourse of resistance. Before discussing the stories, she checks their recall of these terms, asserting her authority, declaring what terms will be used to talk about the story (1). Victoria somewhat offhandedly defines discourses of resistance as a 'whole lot of words' and recalls the discussion they had had about freedom to be sexy and attractive. At the age these girls are (ten and eleven), 'sexy and attractive' are part of the repertoire of resistance to adult-imposed definitions of childhood. However, Chas construes Victoria as having misheard the question or misunderstood the concept and points out that 'sexy and attractive' are part of the dominant (adult) discourse on femininity, again asserting her right to define the question and what constitutes a correct answer (4). Victoria tries to retrieve her position as one who knows by asserting that one should not have to be feminine in that way, that is one can resist such impositions. Alison then seizes power, commenting on Chas's bra and, by implication, her achievement of herself as sexy and attractive (6–8). She thus returns the conversation to the direction Victoria originally took it in. Victoria joins in this disruption to Chas's agenda, though constituting Alison as intrusive of Chas's privacy, thus working on the friendship she wants with Chas (10). Chas returns the discussion to discourses of resistance and tries to get the girls to think how to resist the imposition of dominant discourses on transforming oneself into a sex object (11–17). The girls list some of the features of ruling-class femininity, presumably because they experience them as powerful and as precluding the constitution of themselves as sex objects, which, as they revealed in other conversations, they saw as happening to working-class girls (18–21).

Again, because Chas is focused on gender, she does not hear the talk as about class relations any more than she heard the earlier talk as about adult–child relations.

When she rejects the girls' offerings they come up with another dualism, that of culture/nature. If a girl can't be what people are pushing her into being then she could be 'natural' (23). When Chas starts to elaborate what natural might mean, they associate naturalness with ugliness and so reject naturalness, having placed it within the binary pair of beautiful/ugly. The girl who is not successfully pretty, who wants to be that natural thing 'herself', a wish they acknowledge as proper (30), is nevertheless only imaginable as ugly, even monstrous, having pimples and under-arm hair that comes down to her legs.

The discourses available to these girls enable them to talk about themselves and femininity in powerful ways. They presume their privileged position will protect them from any attacks they might be subjected to if they are perceived as being too overtly sexual. While they talk about the appropriateness of dressing up in sexy ways to attract boys, this is very carefully defined so as not to involve stepping outside their privileged class position (Davies 1993). At the same time as the girls constitute themselves as other to working class, they also define themselves as other to male.

The girls' conversation thus involves displays of the knowledges they have of how to be correctly positioned in terms of gender and class. These form an unquestioned background to their positioning of themselves as rebellious students and friends of Chas. What it is that she wants to teach them is not really something they want or are able to hear, in large part because of the assumptions they each make about the way schooling is done. Further, if gender is not as central to their readings of themselves as class is, their gender is, in some important senses, unmarked for them and therefore not something they are able to construe as a problem. Curthoys (1991) talks about the difficulty that any of us have in holding class and gender and ethnicity simultaneously in any analytic frame; we tend to be able to talk about one of these, or, at most, two in any particular scene. Curthoys likens this to the problem scientists had in describing the relations between the earth and the moon and the sun, the three-way influence long escaping their analytic powers. In the case of an excerpt such as the above, or indeed in any work with children, we need to add in adult–child relations, authority relations and friendship as potentially part of the dynamic interplay between any two people, or any group of people.

Oppressive gendered practices are generally not intentional acts of oppression. More often than not they are invisible to the oppressors because they are inherent in ways of speaking-as-usual. Discourses are made visible in school, not as constitutive practices, but because, according to the more usual ways of thinking about language in school contexts, there are 'correct' and 'incorrect' ways of describing and analysing what is taken to be real. Teachers' own discursive practices, however, are not usually subjected to critical scrutiny. They are under-stood simply as the way teaching is normally done, or the particular way in which a certain set of educational aims are achieved.

Those who are in a position to assess teachers usually do so in the same way teachers assess students, that is in terms of the correctness or incorrectness of their ways of speaking/teaching. If a particular teacher's practices become the topic of conversation, they are usually legitimated (described in terms of) the normative order, or a set of educational aims. When a new discourse is added to the field of educational discourses, such as the gender–equity discourse, teachers are not given the opportunity to examine how their teaching-as-usual might constitute the very patterns of gender relations that the new discourse calls in question. They are, therefore, not given the opportunity to resolve the dilemmas that arise when one set of ideals legitimates and condones the very practices that bring about the outcomes that are called into question by a different set of aims (Clark 1989). Poststructuralist theory provides a set of analytic tools that make it possible to examine teaching-as-usual and its constitutive effects. As well, it opens up the opportunity, in thinking quite differently about what we do, to develop a new set of practices that disrupt old authorities and certainties, that rid us of stereotypical thinking, and open up the possibility of creating something new. The analysis of the conversation with Chas and the St Clement's group provides an important backdrop to such claims however, revealing as it does the force of the known existing structures.

What I want to do in this chapter is to examine some strategies I have used to work with students to enable them and me to see the kinds of things discussed in the earlier chapters, to see how we ourselves are constituted through discourse, coerced by it, and yet made into speaking subjects who can begin to disrupt and move beyond coercive patterns we do not want. The two strategies I will look at are collective biography in which students examine their own biographical texts, and the examination of popular texts written/produced by others. In this instance, I will use the film *Pretty Woman*.

My purpose in this chapter, then, is to explore ways of working in classrooms that allow us to subject texts to critical scrutiny, to locate their constitutive force. In doing so, I make relevant the taken-for-granted knowledges of the reader/viewer, since these are fundamental to the force of the text. The chapter examines the ways in which the constitutive force of texts can be disrupted by making visible that which is usually taken-for-granted, while, at the same time, revealing the complexity of the ways in which realities are held in place by social structure, and by each individual's psychic/bodily specificity (embedded in particular discourses about what it means to be a person). Again, as in chapter 2, this chapter shows how what is see-able depends on the availability of particular discourses, one's positioning within them, the particular context, the social structure and each person's specific history of being in the world.

A central strategy in coming to understand the constitutive force of discourse/text is to examine the multiple possible readings of any text and how they are arrived at. At the same time, I will explore the use of text, or readings of text, to disrupt powerful, dominant discourses and to establish others. I will do this using Barthes' distinction between pleasure and bliss. The pleasurable experience of text is to do with 'understanding' it, knowing how it is created and how it satisfies. It is to do with membership, belonging, having a place within a knowable, predictable social world. Bliss is to do with movement beyond what is known and predictable, it is the creation of an edge, the other side of which is escape from the stultifying coercive nature of the familiar. It is to do with disruption, with madness, with making the marginal central.

Collective biography

Collective biography or memory work is the most powerful strategy I know for breaking open the objective/subjective binarism. 'Objectivity', as we understand that term, involves peeling off 'irrelevancies' so that one can arrive at a set of statements about some aspect of 'reality', a set of statements that is systematic, consistent (both internally consistent and consistent with other 'truths'), and convincing (both to the author and to those actual and imagined readers s/he deems relevant). It presumes the independent existence of that reality from any statement about it or theory of it. What is deemed irrelevant becomes invisible—such as the scientist who conducts the experiment (or his or her gender, motivations, political commitments and private agendas). The version of reality that might have emerged if a different set of relevancies had been attended to takes on a non-existent quality. The scientific discourse that is used to frame the experiment goes so far as to make the detail of those other possibilities not only irrelevant, but non-sensical. Apart from the occasional radical thinker who breaks such bounds (and is more often than not denounced and derided for doing so), each new scientist can only give free reign to their imagination within the range of what is made thinkable by the discourses that have been deemed relevant.

Collective biography or 'memory work' is not only a strategy that can be used in courses on feminist theory and practice, as I have done, but a strategy that can be used by any group of people struggling to relate feminist poststructuralist theory to experience of being gendered. It was developed by Frigga Haug and her associates and reported in *Female Sexualization* (Haug *et al.* 1987). It involves the writing of stories that are, in the first instance, autobiographical, but which become the basis of collective biographies—stories which encapsulate a truth for everyone in the group, and which have moved beyond a statement about the particular individual who wrote the story, to a revelation of the social and discursive processes through which we become individuals. As Barthes says of text:

> *Text* means *Tissue*; but whereas hitherto we have always taken this tissue as a product, a ready made veil, behind which lies, more or less hidden, meaning (truth), we are now emphasizing, in the tissue, the generative idea that the text is made, is worked out in a perpetual interweaving; lost in this tissue—this texture—the subject unmakes himself, like a spider dissolving in the constructive secretions of its web. Were we fond of neologisms, we might define the theory of the text as an *hyphology* (*Hyphos* is the tissue and the spider's web).

(Barthes 1989, p. 64)

Haug's strategy is one in which students/researchers can work to see the tissue, can spin the web of themselves and find themselves in the act of that spinning, in the process of making out of the cultural threads through which lives are made. They can examine the construction of their own biography as something at the same time experienced as personal and their own—woven out of their own body/minds—and yet visibly made out of, even determined by, materials and practices not originating from them.

The basic steps for developing a collective biography that I have developed, following a reading of *Female Sexualization*, are as follows. There are obviously many variations that each group working on collective biography can develop, depending on the requirements of their topic and the background of the participants. The workshops I have run have mostly been with students familiar with poststructuralist theory and with Haug *et al.*'s book:

1 The group who have agreed to work together on a memory project meet to choose a topic which will form the basis of their memory work. This might be a topic such as the acquisition of genderedness, or the embodiment of oneself as male or female, or it might be to do with the acquisition of such emotions as shame or guilt, or an analysis of specific discourses such as the discourse of romantic love, and one's positioning within it. The group then discusses the topic they have chosen in terms of the cultural knowledges through which sense is usually made of the topic—the hegemonic versions of it[2] and their own remembered stories in relation to it. This may take several meetings.

2 Each individual then chooses one or more of the remembered stories that they have talked about as the key episodes that they wish to focus on.

3 The 'owners' of those stories then write them down and read them to the group. In doing so, each writer aims to tell their experience as it was at the time, as far as that is possible. Judgments and explanations that seem relevant in the present and which serve to locate the writer as the person in the present, rather than the person in the past who is being written about, are shed as far as possible.

4 The group discusses these written memories in terms of their own experiences and in terms of any relevant cultural resources available on the topic. The owner of the story uses these discussions as the basis of further drafts of the story until such time as the rationalisations, explanations and justifications have been peeled away and a story is told which might have been true for anyone living in that particular culture and taking up that culture as their own.

What happens in the discussions around the successive drafts of each person's story is particularly fascinating and varies both from one group to another and from one story to another. Sometimes the draft of the story needs no further writing since

---

[2]   I use the scientist here for my example because of the hegemony of what is known as science in our culture. Of hegemony Fraser says:

'Hegemony' is the Italian Marxist Antonio Gramsci's term for the discursive face of power. It is the power to establish the 'common-sense' or 'doxa' of a society, the fund of self-evident descriptions of social reality that go without saying. This includes the power to establish authoritative definitions of social situations and social needs, the power to define the universe of legitimate disagreement, and the power to shape the political agenda. Hegemony, then, expresses the advantaged position of dominant social groups with respect to discourse. (Fraser 1992, p. 179)

all the re-thinking that needed to be done was done in the discussion prior to the first writing. In the bathtub story which I wrote about in *Shards of Glass,* both the writer and the collective biography group were satisfied with the story in its first telling. My discussion of that story went as follows:

> [Jean's] collective biography story ... provides an explicit example of desire being shaped in accordance with the gender categories to which one finds oneself assigned. It is also possible to see how apparently innocent *practices* which presuppose a gendered social structure can play a significant part in recreating that gendered structure. It is in the particular moment captured by this story, that her brother's penis specifically comes to be associated with his competence, dominance and power. The binary discourses through which her subjectification takes place make her brother's power specifically not her own, since, as girl, she is other-than-male, other-than-one-who-is-powerful. She achieves herself in this moment as girl. That is, she achieves herself as not powerful, and more significant, as *not desiring* power.

> I don't remember exactly how old I am, but I must have been pretty young because my brother, Max, and I still took baths together. Each night we would urinate before going into the tub. I had never expressed any interest before, but tonight I realized how fascinating it was that Max could urinate standing up. I watched with obvious delight as he controlled the direction and force of the flow and pretended to bomb submarines in the toilet. He was clearly enjoying himself, and, as always, I wanted to play. I threw pieces of paper in the toilet and Max soaked them instantly. When it came to be my turn to urinate, I decided to try it standing up, like Max. I didn't know quite how to position myself. First I tried standing up just as Max had, but my little trickle missed the bowl completely. Then I tried squatting over the toilet. This time I managed to get it all in, but not with anywhere near the same amount of force and accuracy Max had exhibited. I most certainly couldn't aim at targets like he had, and I didn't have a penis to hold on to to control my stream. Whatever it was that I had, and I didn't know the name of it, was clearly inadequate. I was envious of the power and control Max had over his genitals. I was disappointed that we could only play the game when he was around, too. I cleaned up the floor and we got in the tub.

> While we played in the tub that evening, my attention was predominantly focused on Max's penis. There it was in plain view. I felt different from him tonight, unlike I ever had. He assumed his usual position in the back of the tub so he could slide down on the incline and create waves for his toy boats. The object of his game was to shoot down any of my toys with his, or to go under the water for a sneak attack. Maybe it was just because he was bigger, older, and stronger, but he always managed to win. I felt dominated by him, almost powerless. The only way I could win was by outsmarting him, and then he would cheat. No matter how hard I tried, I'd never win. Why should I even bother to try?

> (Collective biography workshop)

85

Apparently harmless social rituals such as that of males urinating standing up and females urinating sitting down, combined with the binary divisions in the discourses through which male and female subjectivities are achieved, can thus be seen to constitute the experience of male superiority and female inferiority. The boy's penis is something that is named, recognised, touchable and usable, not only for urinating but also for play, and, in this case, for powerful play, making clear the usually symbolic connection between penises and powerful destructive missiles. This particular practice provides Max with a powerful subject position that he can take up, with his penis as central to that power. He *recognises* himself as powerful and uses that power in the ensuing play. In contrast, Jean's attempt at urinating standing up or squatting fail. She has no named, known, touchable part of herself that she can use in her efforts: 'Whatever it was that I had, and I didn't know the name of it, was clearly inadequate'. Jean's lack of aim seemed 'natural', that is, to do with the physiology of her body. She did not realise boys' aim is the result of much practice, often with not very successful outcomes, and that girls can learn to hold their labia in such a way that their aim and force is at least equal to any boy's. Without access to this information and this practice, her powerlessness was understood in relation to an absence, a lack, a no-name.

> Silence itself—the things one declines to say, or is forbidden to name, ... is less the absolute limit of discourse, the other side from which it is separated by a strict boundary, than an element that functions alongside the things said, with them and in relation to them within over-all strategies.
>
> (Foucault 1980, p. 27)

Haug *et al.*, writing about the collective biography or memory work they undertook in Germany, also discuss silence and, in particular, the silences that surround female genitals. Following a story in which a girl talks about the struggle to learn to keep her legs together as 'good girls' should, Haug *et al.* say:

> Clearly, then, something 'sexual' is being signified through leg posture. In expending such large amounts of energy on keeping our legs together, we begin to feel there is something we must keep hidden ... It is through the activity of concealment that meaning is generated ... 'Sexualization' is acquired without sexuality itself ever being mentioned.
>
> (Haug *et al.* 1987, p. 77)

Thus the lack of naming, this sense of absence created around female genitalia is also fundamental to the social practices through which femaleness is constituted.

> (Davies 1993, pp. 27–9)

In that same group with Jean was Peter, a young man who clung to what he took to be a correct version of his story, according to standards quite other than those of collective biography. What for him was hegemonic—scientific discourse, rational explanation, his location of himself as male—were visibly present. His story was a means of revealing these features in himself and was fairly undeveloped if these features were peeled away. The group discussions made visible the way his current positioning of himself was interfering with the story, and the ways in which his mode of telling had blurred, rather than made clear, the story to be told. The aim of such discussions is to enable each writer to move on to successive re-writings of the story that allow more detail of the experience, as it was at the time, to be retrieved *and*, at the same time, begin to ring true to all members of the group as a story through which their understanding of the process under scrutiny can be furthered. This requires that the ways in which the discourses through which gender is constructed, and is being constructed in the story, be made visible, both as these appear in the original experience and in the current construction of it. Haug *et al.* say of this process:

> In challenging each other and ourselves to work with our memories, we were confronted with the problem of the uniqueness or singularity of any given experience. Since it is as individuals that we interpret and suffer our lives, our experiences appear unique and thus of no value for scientific analysis. The mass character of social processes is obliterated within the concept of individuality. Yet we believe that the notion of the uniqueness of experience and of the various ways in which it is consciously assessed is a fiction. The number of possibilities for action open to us is radically limited. We live according to a whole series of imperatives: social pressures, natural limitations, the imperative of economic survival, the given conditions of history and culture. Human beings produce their lives collectively. It is within the domain of collective production that individual experience becomes possible. If therefore a given experience is possible, it is also subject to universalisation.

(Haug *et al.* 1987, pp. 43–4)

Some of the ways in which Haug's group worked to discover the ways in which their stories revealed the 'mass character of social process', rather than their own specificity, were as follows:

> The first step in analysis thus involved all members of the group expressing their opinions and judgements; in addition, they studied the theories, popular sayings, images and so on that already surrounded their object: in other words, the way in which the field was already colonized. We encountered evidence of a huge discrepancy between what we normally take to be our theoretically well-founded, enlightened and radical way of thinking, and our spontaneous judgements and feelings on the events of our childhood ... A particularly productive stage of our work was thus the phase in which we analyzed the way in which our consciousness becomes ideologized, through noting down all the interpretative models, feelings, thoughts, snippets of popular wisdom, judgements, that we and others might bring to each story.

(Haug *et al.* 1987, p. 59)

Along with this examination of the texts produced by each participant, Haug's group undertook to search out any relevant historical documents, old and new doctrines and dogma, images and fairytales, proverbs and newspaper articles. Next, they looked again at their own texts to examine the words they had used to tell of their experiences, to tell the ways in which their experiences were ensnared within the words they used. Were there other words, other ways of telling the events that removed them from the assumptions of the present ? In its final stages, Haug's group often moved over to a use of the third person in their telling of the story and they included in their telling the perspectives of the other characters in their stories:

> Many of our stories derive their initial plausibility from the apparent incomprehensibility of the action of others. Just as in fairytales the plot is carried forward by the actions of the good and bad fairies, we too view the character traits of others as decisive in directing our lives—even though we have long since stopped 'believing' in fairy tales. People act in particular ways, we say, because they are 'evil'; intrinsically 'bad'; mothers are petty, school friends envious and hateful, and so on. In depicting others in this way, we are however, likely to be disguising our own contradictions—or at least attempting to construct them into some sort of unity. Ideas of this kind paralyze us in our daily lives. In analyzing our stories we therefore found it necessary to provide detailed descriptions of other protagonists, to represent their actions from the point of view of their own interests and motives. Just as we became capable of producing a complete description of ourselves by virtue of a simple process of distancing (writing in the third person), it was equally simple to write credible motives for the actions of others into the revised versions of our stories. The transformation this effected was no more or less than revolutionary and what we learned from it is incalculable.

> (Haug *et al.* 1987, p. 70)

The process of unfolding versions of the story told by Peter, the young man mentioned above, makes a fascinating story in itself, and illustrates some of the struggle that Haug's group is analysing here. The group of which Peter and Jean were members was formed as part of a course on the acquisition of gender that I taught in the USA. The students in the course undertook to work together on a memory-work project, and to work specifically on the topic of the acquisition of gender. We decided to work on our first memories of being gendered—that is to look for the first conscious point at which we 'knew' we were male or female. There was one male student in the group and there were four female students. The female students had read Haug's book, but Peter, the male student, had not yet got around to it when we began our project. At first the memories were of adolescence and puberty, but we gradually began to retrieve earlier and earlier memories. I worked as a member of the group with stories to tell, and became caught up, as they were, in the process of making visible through those stories—and an examination of the discourses which informed their telling—the ways in which we each had been 'mass produced'. Two members of the group, including Peter, were of Asian background and so we might have been called a culturally diverse group, but the gulf that separated male from female in our comprehension of stories and of the process we were caught up in was far wider than the gulf that separated east from west.

When we first wrote our stories, the young women in the group wrote carefully and at length the stories they had told. Peter, in contrast, wrote very briefly about a

88

memory that he had not previously discussed with the group. When it came to his turn to read his story, he displayed extreme embarrassment and needed some persuasion and support before he could read it. He knew very well the power of his story to offend women, as it has on each of the occasions I have used it since. But there, in the group, there was no offence. Rather, there was a very 'feminine' supporting of his right to speak combined with a genuine fascination for the revelations that his story might hold about the mystery of masculinity, that (more usually) unmarked condition.

Peter's first story was as follows. I have numbered each sentence to aid in the discussion of it:

1   My earliest memory of my being male began with sexual socialization and I remember quite vividly how I become aroused at the sight of a nude woman.

2   Whether it was a sociological conditioning or just my lascivious nature that got me aroused, I will never truly know.

3   Be that as it may, my reaction made me realize—much later in life, of course—that I was male incarnate for responding in the fashion that I did.

4   Funny, however, is that when I went skinny dipping with boys and girls I never reacted similarly.

5   This was probably due to the fact that the girls I was swimming nude with were not fully developed, although I knew that they were female and I was male, nonetheless.

6   Then, anatomy played a major role in making me realise male personal gender.

Apart from his extreme embarrassment in the reading of the story, the most notable feature of this first story is its essential brevity—'I became aroused at the sight of a nude woman' (1) and 'when I went skinny dipping with boys and girls I never reacted similarly' (4). The remainder is essentially explanation and concerned with establishing the presence of Peter as an adult narrator, as male incarnate and as (male) student who can use the academic discourses through which the 'truth' can be ascertained. He overlays the story with 'scientific' explanations, thus distancing himself well and truly from the child he is telling the story about, telling far more, in fact, about who he takes himself to be in the present. He defines the event as 'sexual socialization' (1), then proffers two competing theories to explain the event, one of conditioning and the other of his actual 'nature' (2). He assumes that one of these is a true explanation, but that it is not possible to find out which (2). But he then shows the way in which he has used the event to interpret himself in the present— as 'male incarnate'—that is, as 'real' male. His sex/gender is not in question, because this early event tells him so (3). He is puzzled by lack of similar experiences with young girls—could this cast doubt on his maleness? (4) But no, the explanation is readily found—they were not fully developed (5). His conclusion is that male genitals and their capacity for erection are central in the formation of his male genderedness rather than, presumably, any process of 'conditioning' (6). The story is, in a sense, offered as proof that the masculinity that he is often defensive about in feminist discussions is, in fact, 'natural' and, thus, not something he can be called to account for. As such, Peter writes his story only in small part about the memory of realising he was male. In larger part, it is taking up the many arguments we have had in the class about male and female genderedness. He is using the story as a way of developing an argument that sex/gender is natural rather than acquired.

The group was fascinated by this story. It seemed to offer an insight into the process of male subjectification which was so foreign and inaccessible to the rest of the group. We bombarded him with questions. How old had he been? Where had it happened? How did he feel at the time? We looked at the words he was using and the work they were doing to locate his present self in the story and to overlay it with rationalisation and explanation, and at how these served to obscure his telling of the story, rather than to clarify it. No-one in the group (except, of course, Peter) felt it was a story to be embarrassed about. We encouraged him to write it in more detail, peeling off the layers of explanation and trying to retrieve the experience as it had been then, rather than allowing the discursive production of the person he now takes himself to be to interrupt that telling.

The task set for the next meeting was a rewriting of the stories they each had written. Because our meetings were three- to four-hour meetings, much had been achieved in the first session. When we reconvened Peter's rewritten story was as follows:

1   I remember when I was about three or four years old: it was during that time when I first truly discovered what it was to be male; though my articulation of that memory is far more advanced now than it was back then. In any case, I was living in Korea at the time, and it was fashionable for women to publicly bathe together in a 'bath house'. What's more, it was also orthodox to take an infant or very young child with you when going to one of these bathhouses.

2   So here I was in this bath house with all these nude women surrounding me so nonchalantly, as if it were the most natural thing in the world; actually though it was natural since I was so young. As I began to gape at the wonderful view in front of my eyes, I began also to entertain thoughts that many adults don't think children are capable of thinking. Be that as it may, I kept imagining myself having intercourse with one or more of the ladies in my immediate vicinity. With this in mind, I realized—I think it was more on a subconscious level—that my reaction to the nude women was my way of expressing my masculinity or maleness.

3   What bothers me, however, was whether my reaction was conditioned or was it a natural response considering my sex. I feel in some way that my response could have been conditioned by society, and thus, my reaction was rather reflexive instead of intrinsic. On the other hand, I felt my reaction could have also been instinctive since I truly felt my urges to be solely erotic which stemmed from an innate source.

90

4   My arousal caused a particular anatomical organ to distend profusely. As a result, I quickly looked around for the nearest cold water bath and proceeded to jump in it as quickly as convention allowed. Though I was embarrassed about the whole ordeal, since I knew instinctively that I wasn't supposed to be excited by the presence of nude women at that age, I nonetheless felt that I had expressed my superlative masculinity.

In the first sentence of the first paragraph, he announces a 'true discovery' of his own maleness, then distances himself explicitly from the four-year-old child, explaining that what he can say now is different from what he could have said then. Having thus signalled his awareness of the scientific attitude that might lead to accusations of his fabricating the story, he explains where he was and how the event came about. He was in a women's bathhouse and it was quite usual for children to be there.

In the second paragraph, the context is further elaborated. Then we are given the first dilemma of the story—that it is natural for women to be naked in the presence of innocent children, but that this child was not innocent. His fantasies were adult fantasies. The technical, formal words used to describe those fantasies ('having intercourse with one or more of the ladies in my vicinity') still hold the event away from us, thus making it unreal. In the third sentence, he uses scientific explanation—'subconsciously' he was 'expressing his maleness' through his fantasies—to resolve the first dilemma.

In the third paragraph, he raises the second dilemma of the story, a dilemma that particularly bothers him. Is the 'expression of maleness' achieved through a natural bodily response or has he learned it ? He concedes the possibility of 'society' being the originating force, as so much of the theory in the course he is studying would suggest, but he *experienced* it as coming from himself. This he undoubtedly takes to be a strong argument, since experience is given a privileged place in the many humanist discourses he has been exposed to in his studies.

The fourth paragraph returns to the story and the first dilemma—he had an erection looking at nude women, which, as a child, he should not have done. He was embarrassed and jumped in a cold water bath, feeling nonetheless that he had expressed his 'superlative masculinity'.

This second version of the story caused a further flood of questions and discussion. How did he know to jump in the cold water at the age of four, one of the members of the group asked disbelievingly. Why does he keep distancing himself from the child as if he is ashamed of him? Why does he keep trying to explain instead of just telling us the story? Peter protested at this. His writing would be of no value if he didn't seek to explain. As student, it was the explanations that were of value not the trivial details of his life. As Haug says 'our experiences appear unique and thus of no value for scientific analysis' (Haug *et al.* 1987, p. 43). Haug points out, however, that this kind of discussion is a particularly productive element of memory work, since it is through such discussions that we become aware of the way our tellings of events are unwitting tellings of ourselves and our value positions, rather than of the story. The exercise of separating out the event from the explanatory frameworks through which the event is remembered and told is thus fascinating on several counts: we see the way in which our everyday tellings of events are loaded with values, assumptions and rationalisations about the nature of the world; we see the way in which our tellings are more tellings of ourselves in the present than they are tellings of our past experiences as they were at the time; and we discover the possibility of profound shifts in the perception of events as we become aware of the way in which the words we choose shape the telling of our stories.

It was readily observable that the other members of the group were not as resistive as Peter to retrieving the detail of their own stories and to peeling off the rationalisations and explanations. They expressed fascination with the task at hand and eagerness to pursue it. Their more extensive reading, their greater ease in a feminist course and their 'female genderedness' may each have contributed to this greater ease. Because of Peter's position in the group, that is as the only male within a feminist course, the issue of distancing and guilt in particular, needed to be discussed at length. The students had all expressed some anxiety at the beginning of the course at my references to the differences between men and women, as if it were sexist to draw attention to them. It had taken them some time to accept that if we are going to understand how genderedness gets put in place and held in place, then we need to look at the detail of the way genderedness is played out. They had eventually accepted that, but Peter, nevertheless, still appeared to be guilty and defensive each time features of masculinity were discussed. Marking a previously unmarked category is not straightforward and can easily lead to anxiety and defensiveness, just as it has for example, amongst white, middle-class women when confronted by 'women of colour'. It seemed to Peter that to mention masculine features in a feminist discussion was, by definition, to have judged them as negative and as something that he, as a man, should be ashamed of. His story indicated that this topic needed more careful discussion.

We discussed the fact that while it might be true that some features of masculinity are, by definition, anathema to many feminists, it was not so of all features of masculinity, and, furthermore, that the fascination for examining the detail of the way gender is done was of more interest to us in relation to the topic at hand than the moral judgments we might want to make in other contexts. The fact that his story showed the way the male gaze which constitutes woman as object is the same gaze through which he achieves his sense of his own superior masculinity, was not something to be objected to in this context, but something which allowed us to see what 'discovering' oneself as male is about. Only if he had behaved in patriarchal or destructively male ways within the group would we have felt called upon to take up a radical feminist position and call the acceptability of male interactive styles into account. This discussion was critical in making it discursively possible for Peter to 'own' the story and to cease trying to use it as part of an argument in defence of his own masculinity.

As well, the group discussed a number of strategies for retrieving the details of their stories. One that Peter found particularly productive was to think of the smells and colours of the scene as a way of gaining access to the event as he had experienced it at the time. We further discussed Haug's recommendation that the stories be told in the third person and that attention be paid to the other people in the story, in terms of imagining what the event was about from their perspectives. At first Peter rejected this as 'non-scientific', since he did not 'know' what the other people had thought or felt. He nevertheless agreed to play with the idea in order to get into his story more fully. As Haug predicts, he found that it opened up the story in quite significant ways.

The next draft of his story was, with one small amendment, the final draft. When Peter read out this story, the group sat around spellbound. He was clearly very pleased with what he had written. The group, including Peter, felt that the story was a collective telling of a first awareness of maleness. We could imagine, in listening to the story, just what that experience had been like. Interestingly, it also can be read as a display of Peter as male in the present, displaying his masculine, powerful sexuality to a group of women:

> It was a sultry, steamy, sweltering bathhouse filled with identical rows of bathing pools, both hot and cold. The symmetry and architecture automatically labelled this as a public bathing facility for women. The angular tiles on the walls and floor were less austere so as to give it a feminine quality. The shape of the pools were oval instead of rectangular, and in this way one could not confuse the bathhouse with masculinity. More noticeable, however, was the undeniable aroma of matriarchal gathering—that irrefutable scent of decaying honey produced by the combination of various perfumes and colognes intermixing as one. Some women were strewn here and there haphazardly with their young cherubic children, while others were gathered in small groups whiling away their time with idle gossip. It was not too surprising to have found women lying on marble benches that were permanently embedded into the wall; and these same women lying casually with legs spread and arms behind their heads with their fingers intertwined.

> Altogether, it was a familiar scene: women either bathing or relaxing and children either playing in the bathing pools or staring innocently at whatever caught their fancy. Or so it seemed. For this one particular four-year-old, it was a completely different story, though his perceptions were identical to the described atmosphere of the bathhouse. But his imagination transcended the expected limitations of a young child's fantasy and logic. The first amazement the precocious four-year-old received upon entering the bathhouse was the sight of so many women, but it wasn't just that they were women, indeed no, it was that all the women were fully and casually nude, including his mother, that shocked him so.

> After Peter (the four-year-old) overcame his initial shock, his first conscious effort was to forcibly control the swelling of his phallus since he too was nude, and it would be quite noticeable if there was an obvious swelling of his organ. Peter's mother took him by the hand and guided him to a bench. She told him he could play with the other children but not to upset any of the other women. After that, Peter was left to his own devices, which meant that he could dream and fantasize all he wanted to about the exciting sight before him; namely the nude women.

> Since Peter wanted to get a better view of his main attraction, he went over to his mom who was talking to a group of women, and casually insinuated his presence into their group. He achieved this by gently clasping his

93

mother's hand palm first over his left hand, and with the thumb of his right hand he simply put it into his mouth to give him the verisimilitude of innocence. Having everyone believe in the purity of his mind, Peter began to discreetly look at the women in front of him. After all, since his head came no higher than the waist of the tallest women there, how could anyone ever suspect his mischievous glances? Insofar as the women were concerned, this young child was naive and innocent. However, the truth of the matter was that Peter was intently gazing at the ebony hair between the legs of the women in the group, and he did so by making it look as if he were looking at the floor. Furthermore, the steam did a lot to hide Peter's secretive glances.

A point of critical interest for Peter, and a most erotic scene, was the glistening beads of sweat and water slowly meandering their way down the breast and stomach of one particular woman; the bead of hot water snaking its way into the ebony forest of her passion—the passion (heat) caused by the sultry atmosphere of her environment. Moreover, the bead was impelled to explore its forest until ultimately, it found itself hanging by one tenuous hair; for it then hung precariously for a second or so until it fell as if it were captured in midair for a fleeting moment before plunging into a puddle of water causing a silent but mentally audible 'splash!' The beads reminded Peter of drops of nectar dripping off the edge of a split pomegranate, and thus, the beginning of his masculinity via sexual awareness began in that steamy bathhouse.

There were women sitting in manly postures, legs spread apart, revealing much for the curious. Other positions included women laying down with one arm behind the head, the other arm resting upon her stomach, and one leg bent at the knee so that her raised leg assumes a ninety degree angle. Be that as it may, Peter found the latter posture entirely stimulating. He imagined himself assuming the position of an adult male who ingratiates himself to this woman lying on her back. Soon after, Peter's imagination culminates into a sexual frenzy with this woman, but with him being on top.

While in the course of his imagined intercourse, some deep emotions are peaked within Peter. He comes to realize the difference between masculinity and femininity—between male and female, but from an infantile perspective. He feels the dominant nature of maleness and believes in its superiority, and further, he takes uncanny pride in being male. His revelation began with the picture of two boys or two men in a brawl. The winner of these fights normally claims victory by remaining on top of his opponent, and thus pins the loser down until he concedes the match. This vivid image of dominance attributed to the person on top of the weaker opponent plays an important role in influencing Peter's vision of dominance. Similarly, it is traditional for the man to assume the dominant role by mounting the woman, and hence, he is the superior gender for being on top. More important, however, is that Peter juxtaposes fights between two boys or two men with sexually male-dominant acts; and furthermore, by superimposing this scene of male on top of the male, and the male on top of the female, he rationalizes this to be dominance and superiority in its true essence.

As the steam thickened in the bathhouse, perceptions got warped and visibility became difficult, but for Peter, the steam became a shield for his

94

erection. To forestall undue embarrassment Peter realized that he would need a means of escape so he could not only deflate his erection but he could also keep his passions in check. The cold bath opposite of the hot baths became the answer for his dilemma. He quickly but discreetly made his way over to the cold baths. No sooner had he jumped in the cold water when he realized that his phallus instantly shrank to its smallest superlative size. Thus his ardor remained in check for the remainder of his stay at the bathhouse.

As for the other children, they too seemed to be busy with their imaginations, but like all cunning children, they are very adept at maintaining their innocence. Incidentally, it never occurred to Peter to place any importance on the faces of the women present in the bathhouse. This was partially due to steam obscuring any details of the women's faces, and partially due to the unimportance of a face because the body signified whether a person was male or female (besides the fact that he was in an all female bathhouse), and thus Peter's sole concern was for the physical attributes of the women rather than their complexion.

For the remainder of his stay at the bathhouse, Peter remained complacently in the cold water, for he came to realize, through his own rationalization, his own dominance in the world of gender awareness. And oddly enough, he felt rather relieved to know that he was a male and not a female, as if by not being female he just escaped a dreary life of drudgery.

In this version of his story, Peter had successfully peeled away the rationalisations of the present, the display of himself as student, and had achieved a telling that satisfied him and that seemed to us, as women, to have given us an insider's view of that experience. But he had managed at the same time to display himself as male through erotic imagery—the poetics of male sexuality. So successfully had he done this that I noticed Jean giving him quite 'smouldering' looks, which quite startled me at the time, given what I regarded as the quite appalling revelations in his story about the nature of masculinity with its imagery in which violence, dominance, superiority and a positive sense of male sexuality were imbricated one with another. Another way of describing what was happening in this mixing of past and present would be to say that in discovering and talking about what it meant to be male, through his story, he got caught up in being the very thing he was talking about.

In a slightly different context, Orr addresses this problem, talking about the (almost) impossible nature of the task of understanding theory without being taken over by it:

> But in pursuing the recognizably sociological project of weaving autobiography and history, of investigating the complex cultural text(ure)s of individual consciousness and social structures, I am also trying to do something more. Or less. In contrast to most sociological techniques for storytelling, I am interested in finding a practice of writing that evokes the political imperative, but also the *impossibility* of writing our social bodies in relation to their multiple levels of determination. I am interested in feminist social research that reflexively demonstrates the social, historical, and autobiographical conditions under which it is produced. Conditions that produce a text, 'my own', full of gaps, excesses, anger, uncertainty, desire,

fragments, and traces of the banal and dramatic violence of working in a language that, theoretically and socially, I refuse to call 'my own'.

(Orr 1990, p. 482)

A very different collective biography workshop was with a group of Australian postgraduate students. They chose menstruation as their topic. This seemed to hold a particularly interesting set of possibilities, of stories not yet told, but perhaps vividly remembered. It seemed, as well, to be of specific interest in relation to the process of becoming female, in this case, adult female. The transition from being child of one's own mother to potential mother of one's own child is marked by the onset of menstruation and is therefore a powerful moment of transition between one category and another. It is at this point that a girl is often handed by her mother some of the fundamental stories that she must incorporate in her understanding of what it means to be a woman. Vulnerability to rape, her position within and obligation to the patriarchy can serve to make the transition not a simple celebratory one, nor one in which category boundaries are drawn, but a heavy marking of fear and responsibility accompanied by silence. In *The Woman Warrior* (Kingston 1977), Kingston tells of such a moment at the onset of her own menstruation when her mother tells her of her aunt's rape and subsequent suicide and the imperative of silence surrounding this event:

> 'You must not tell anyone' my mother said, 'what I am about to tell you. In China, your father had a sister who killed herself. She jumped into the family well. We say that your father has all brothers because it is as if she had never been born. ... Don't let your father know that I told you. He denies her. Now that you have started to menstruate, what happened to her could happen to you. Don't humiliate us. You wouldn't like to be forgotten as if you had never been born. The villagers are watchful.

(Kingston 1977 pp. 11, 13)

For Kingston then, menstruation came to signify not so much womanhood or adulthood, but the possibility of becoming no one, should she transgress the rules for female sexual behaviour and become pregnant. The power of her father to negate her aunt's identity and to refuse to speak her name is a fearful possibility for her as well, which holds her into a particular form of femininity passed on to her by her mother, in the name of her father.

Most of us in the group had fairly negative experiences of the onset of menstruation. Only two said that it had been a good experience. All one of us could remember was a grin from ear to ear. In the discussion leading up to the writing of stories I asked her to tell us more about that grin:

> Well it's real, ah I can't, well, at this stage I can't remember all of it. All I can remember is, going to the toilet and discovering blood all over my pants, and, I said to Mum 'is this what it is?' sort of and she said 'yes' and I can remember having this huge grin [pause] all over my face at the fact that I had started, so she must have told me about it in a very positive way I think... (So, so the sort of 'grin' can you talk more about that? How it actually felt?) Well it was excited, I s'pose. It was the start of womanhood, or something, the start of of um growing up yeah a signal of growing up, or

96

something like that. (Is that what it meant to you, do you think?) I think so, well yes I think so. (It wasn't that you could now have babies?) Oh no, nothing like that. Never in that connection. 'Now you're a real woman.' I can remember a lot of people saying things like that.

After listening to the others' stories, however, she chose not to write the story of the grin, but another story that she had forgotten until then that revealed the total ignorance she had of sexuality. On the school bus someone had used the word 'fuck' and she didn't know what it meant. Her story was about asking what it meant and about how embarrassed and ashamed she was at having openly asked someone its meaning. Her positive experience of menstruation had been revealed in the group discussions to her as something that was only possible because of the total silence that had surrounded sexuality to that point.

The other story which tells of the experience of menstruation as positive and open, nevertheless includes an association with sexuality and the male gaze, and the wrongness of allowing one's genitals to be seen:

> It was a puzzle, this stain on my pyjamas and my twin sister and I discussed it and decided that it probably had a simple explanation and was connected with the run of sickness we had been having. My mother found the pants and asked us about them and explained menstruation in such a way that we both had no problems with it. I have no memory what she actually said but I somehow remember that she made me feel a bit special that I was menstruating so young.
>
> A few days later Mum told us that, if we ever began menstruating at school we should see such and such a teacher, and also that two other girls in our class had begun menstruating. So although it was awkward, it was not a problem.
>
> I had always liked my body, but had also been aware that it was somehow dangerous. At the small one-teacher school I attended I remember an older grade seven girl being dared to do backbends and being puzzled by the boys' obvious interest in looking at her pants and also somehow feeling ashamed for her. I also remember being kissed? touched? by one of the older boys when I was alone behind the water tanks and again being puzzled, annoyed, a bit ashamed. I told my sister and my parents whatever they told me or did, I did not feel threatened.
>
> Although I was made aware that boys enjoyed looking at female bodies, I also found my body pleasurable. My twin sister and I played sensual games 'Plucking the Chook', and with my cousins we played having babies, with the best part being the time 'the doctor' touched your genitals as she pulled the baby out.

The initial session, following the story of the grin, was very much taken up with a discussion about secrecy and shame. Even in one school where girls talked openly about menstruating and about who had started or who 'had theirs', there was still a taboo against letting anyone know the particular time when you were menstruating. Bulky pads had to be smuggled to the toilets and care taken that no-one knew. In one story that was told, about a tampon lying in the school grounds, deep shame was experienced:

> I can remember—it was probably about my *third* period at school by now and I had my tampons in my pocket and I was walking up the playground and I had a hole in my blazer pocket and I went up to the Library and I put my hand in my pocket and I just felt the hole—and I was trying to associate what happened and I just felt the hole but I can remember that there was a tampon lying in the playground outside on the ground and there was no tampon in my pocket and all these people were just walking around it and you know there was my tampon *right in the middle* of the playground, walking right around that and I could see that, and I thought 'oh no I don't have any more, I am going to go and have to retrieve that in front of everybody, oh dear'. And when I *finally* got the courage up when no one else was around and go down and find this tampon and *get* it quickly while no one was there and put it in my pocket, I can remember actually doing that and got it into my pocket and I realised my tampons were actually in *my tunic*!! what a traumatic experience.

Interestingly, one of the stories came from a person whose family had traditionally celebrated the onset of menstruation. She had learned independently of her family that such celebration was inappropriate, since secrecy was all important. Armed with such knowledge she was able to resist the celebration of her own menstruation:

> When my sister began to menstruate for the first time, she came to tell me about it and wondered what to do. She was put in this sort of a situation of not knowing what to do because my mother never ever spoke to us about menstruation, sex or childbirth, having to talk to Mum now about menstruation is going to be an uncomfortable encounter.

> I explained to my older sister that she had no option but to mention it to Mum because we did not have pads and the only way to get one was to tell Mum. So she did. Well, Mum made my sister a tall glass of Egg-flip and forced her to drink it saying that she (my sister) had to keep her strength up because she could feel weak with all that bleeding. Then plans were made to celebrate. We invited family over for Sunday lunch and my sister was given gifts. My sister, (as far as I can remember) stayed in her/our room and refused to socialise with the rest of the crowd.

> She must have been embarrassed—I remember discussing this with her and thinking that when it came to my turn, this sort of celebration was not on. I was not going to put up with 'everyone' knowing that I had menstruated for the first time. I am not sure if I had voiced these wishes to my mother or whether fuss was only made of the first female child—but when it was my turn, I mentioned it to my sister who gave me all the appropriate gear to cope with the situation. Amongst ourselves, we must have decided that it would be appropriate to let mother know. I remember the surprise on the faces of female relatives when my mother whispered to them that I had 'become a young lady'. 'At so young an age?' came the reply. I was perhaps 11 or 12 years old then. Yet they all seemed pleased as though I had been promoted for a good deed or something. I could not understand their delight. How

could anyone be happy about bleeding, feeling sick and being in pain. I thought they were all weird and I remember thinking that this is the end of one chapter in my life and the beginning of another – one that I was not looking forward to—a life of pain and having no option but to put up with it.

Intricately tied in with the secrecy, shame and management of menstruation were attitudes to female sexuality and the unnameable, unknown, untouchable features of female genitalia. What begins to emerge fairly rapidly in the stories is that there is little consciousness on the part of the women of distinguishing themselves categorically from men, of, in any sense, recognising that they were being constituted inside the male/female dualism. Rather what emerges is a taking on as their own, knowledge of their bodies as having secretive and shameful parts that are shameful in relation to the male gaze. So carefully must they be hidden from such shaming that very often they were hidden from the young women themselves. I remembered, for example, when I was about eight being asked in a 'significant' tone of voice by my older sister whether I dried myself between my legs after my bath, my sister implying that only bad girls touched themselves 'there'. Closely related to this memory was another of older girls saying that only 'nymphos' used tampons. Another member of the group had a similar memory of her mother instructing her not to touch herself 'there':

> For goodness sake, I could never *wash* myself, 'cause I can remember being a tiny little kid about aged 2 or 3, I have a really long memory, and my mother saying while I was in the bath 'don't touch yourself there, don't touch yourself there, its not nice'. And I bloody never *did*, for twenty years, and I got all these vaginal infections because I didn't wash myself.

The extent to which we took on as our own the moral assumptions of the stories we were told was indicated in my rejoining story:

> I remember going swimming and in the changing rooms—there was a woman who had stripped off her clothes and was actually vigorously drying herself between her legs and I thought this is awful, how could she *do* that? A live nymphomaniac!! She looked like a really ordinary woman and I couldn't see anything sexual about it, but I was *mortified* that she would do it.

The instruction not to touch oneself led some members of the group to know almost nothing about their own anatomy. One story that was told located the bleeding as coming from 'the bottom':

> . . . by an absolute stroke of luck I had a friend at school who wasn't very close, but she must've got her period and in her great, sort of, need to tell someone about it, she got me one day and said 'Do you know that women bleed from the bottom?' And I said 'Um oh yeah, right, right. Oh, well, thanks, see you later'. And she sort of, she kept, she was trying to *tell* me something and I couldn't get what it was. It was, you know, a bit obscure. And so I thought, oh, well right oh. But fortunately that was all I needed to alert me, because sure enough one day I woke up and there I was bleeding from the bottom, and I kind of instinctively knew it wasn't my anus from which I was bleeding. But, you know, 'down there' is all sort of the bottom. So I went in to my mother and said (whispers) 'Mum I'm bleeding from the

bottom' and ah she said '*Oh dear*, you poor little thing, come and get into bed'. And she put me into her bed and, ah, she got me a pad from the wardrobe and so I immediately realized that I had a grave illness for which I didn't have to go to school that day or anything and you know...

The most traumatised memory was one which, like Kingston's story, connected menstruation with death. Death is the most marked feature of the story, but it is interesting to note that all the same features of the previous stories are woven in, but with the twist of death giving them their own particular meaning for the owner of the story. Her first story in the group had been about that silence, in particular, the importance of not talking to men or boys about menstruation. In that first story she recorded her horror when she found out from the books she read that some men did know about it. Her second story was as follows:

I have been upset all day. This morning I bled, for the first time. I was scared and didn't want to tell anyone. After all, they would tell me it is my first step to womanhood, it is a sign that with God's blessing I can become a mother.

But I do not want to become a 'woman' nor a 'mother'. I want to be me. My mother didn't want to be a woman or a mother. She escaped by wallowing in a medicated sleep—I do not want to die early.

Do I have a choice? I must accept that I will bleed regularly unless those internal organs are re-worked. But, I can choose not to become a mother, not to become a housewife, not to have an early death.

Will the bleeding ever stop? I do not like this secrecy about pads and belts— I was told about all these things in a hushed whisper 'Do not talk to men about this'. Why do I keep it secret—am I supposed to be ashamed to be a 'woman'. If it ends in early death, yes, I can see the shame.

OK, I will accept that the bleeding will return every few weeks. But I do not have to accept motherhood or womanhood. They are from the outside. I need not die early.

What emerged for us from these stories, then, was the recognition that menstruation taboos are not experienced as boundary markers only, but as deeply felt elements of *oneself*. We each take up an attitude to the social world from a position strongly defined in terms of who we take ourselves to be. The menstruation taboo effectively constitutes woman as other to man, in part in response to his imagined gaze, but in larger part quite independently of that gaze. She takes on as her own the shame and secrecy associated with her own body and with its reproductive force. The taboo works as a means of category-maintenance work on the category 'woman', in this case, maintaining the meaning of the category by inscribing her body as shameful in the moment of transition into adulthood/womanhood at the very moment when she might otherwise have gained an unequivocal sense of herself as both sexual and powerful. Individual men need do little to oppress individual women once they have taken on, as their own, the discourses about their own body which make it something to be secretive and shameful about. The oppression exists in the bodies as they are discursively constituted in this way. Undoing a taboo thus undoubtedly requires structural/classificatory work on the binarism male/female, but it also involves work on subjectivity—and the associated access to the means to unlock the personal power of the taboo. These stories seemed to us an interesting step towards recognising, and then shedding, some of the negative feelings we found we still had about our bodies, despite our access to feminist discourse. We could think about doing so more readily because we no longer experienced them solely as private and personal but as cultural/discursive productions in which we had been caught up.

Similar in some ways to collective biography were the photography sessions that the primary-school study groups undertook with Chas (cf. also Chappell 1984). The groups worked together to learn to read the semiotic detail of family photographs and then each gathered a photo history of themselves, looking for the ways their gender was being constituted in the representations of themselves that they found there. They then went on to take their own photographs of family and friends and to tell stories about the pictures they had created. In this way, they could learn to see the constitutive force of the ways in which they had been positioned and in which they positioned others. The example in chapter 1 of Zac's positioning of his parents and of his own achievement of himself as male within the male/female binary was drawn from that photographic project.

Reading fictional texts

In looking at texts such as the popular film *Pretty Woman*, we can look at multiple readings to see how viewers constitute (fictional) realities out of the detail of their own constitution as subjects, out of the contexts of their viewing, out of the sets of relevancies they have available to them at that time. Working that way with students allows us to catch ourselves constituting the text and to see the interweaving of multiple fictions/texts (our lives, the lives in the text) to create a particular viewing. It allows us to see how the filling of spaces must be done to achieve any reading and to see how that filling is infinitely multiple. But it also allows us to look at the political nature of the different readings to see how power works through discursive practices, for example in the maintenance of gender and the ascendancy of one gender over another. It is only through detailed multiple readings that this mode of understanding can be achieved.

When *Pretty Woman* first came out it was a box-office success. On the front of the video jacket is a picture of Edward (Richard Gere) and Vivian (Julia Roberts) standing back to back: she in a sexual pose dressed in her hooker gear, he in his business suit, hands in pockets, leaning backwards. She is holding his tie, apparently pulling him towards her: she smiling with amusement, he with a faint, enigmatic smile. The words on the front are 'She walked off the street, into his life and stole his heart'. According to the blurb on the back of the video:

> Roberts stars as a streetwise, down-on-her-luck working girl, whose chance encounter with a handsome corporate mogul leads to an improbable love affair ... and a modern-day Cinderella fantasy that has captured the hearts of movie-goers all over the world... *Pretty Woman* is [an] irresistible romantic comedy that leaves you feeling great!

This would sound like what Barthes calls a 'text of pleasure', rather than a 'text of bliss'. A text of pleasure is one in which all that is familiar is to be repeated in a predictable way:

> Text of pleasure: the text that contents, fills, grants euphoria; the text that comes from culture and does not break with it, is linked to a *comfortable* practice of reading.

(Barthes 1989, p. 14)

A text of bliss in contrast is one that disrupts the familiar:

> Text of bliss: the text that imposes a state of loss, the text that discomforts (perhaps to the point of certain boredom), unsettles the reader's historical, cultural, psychological assumptions, the consistency of his[/her] tastes, values, memories, brings to a crisis his[/her] relation with language.

(Barthes 1989, p. 14)

The film was strongly recommended to me by a friend as a pleasurable film. I watched it with delight, fascinated by the ways in which the film picked up so many of the traditional fairytale romantic storylines and disrupted them in one way or another. In terms of my work with preschool and primary-school children and gender and their hearing of story, this seemed to be a significant film in that it captured the imagination of the viewers through the use of traditional, readily recognised storylines and, at the same time, introduced important feminist shifts in those storylines. The children in the primary-school study groups also talked about how much they had enjoyed it. They talked about how they particularly liked the sexual competence of Vivian and how upset they were when Stuckey (Edward's lawyer) tried to rape her. Their focus, significantly, is not on Vivian's vulnerability and on how wonderful it was that Edward saved her, but on her anger and her struggle to get Stuckey off her. In this reading, Vivian is not a victim but a protagonist who competently moves through the world, defending her right to make choices:

Chas:	Tell me why you like it, what makes it a good story as far as you're concerned?
Tiffany:	Well *Pretty Woman,* it's interesting and it's got sexy women in it (laughter) and she goes 'what colour condom, pink one, purple one, blue one' there's really funny parts in it and it's just really/
Victoria:	Oh that was sad at the end how you know the man who the other man works with, the tall man, you know, the short man how he goes, ... 'If I just screw you'/... and then he goes, 'Screw you' And then he gets on top and she goes 'Get off me get off me!'
Chas:	Oh that was horrible/

Victoria:	I know
Chas:	I hated him
Marcella:	Did you see that?
Chas:	Yes
Marcella:	Oh that was the best movie

(St Clement's, in Davies 1993, p. 120)

But many of the feminists I talked to dismissed the film out of hand as a bad, even dangerous film, even more dangerous if they had caught themselves in the act of enjoying it. If there were any feminist moments in it, then feminism had been colonised and subsumed within the Hollywood version of romance. The dominant text was fantasy/romance of an objectionable kind. It was, they said, a romance that could persuade young women that improbable romances can and do happen and are every bit as much to be longed for as they ever were. Any gestures towards feminism in the film are there simply to seduce the viewer into accepting more readily the old familiar romantic storyline. It reinscribes the fantasy that rich princes do sweep pretty women off their feet and save them from their victim status. Being a sex object is once again made desirable. The film is one that objectifies women offering parts of her body for the male gaze. Furthermore, many of the shots in the film of Vivian's body are reportedly someone else's body, Roberts' body apparently falling short of the perfect sex object status. Looking at the cover on the video, I notice that the body of Vivian is dressed in similar clothes to hers, but they are not hers. The colour is wrong. Presumably this is also not her body.

On reading reviews of the film, I came across one in particular that gave me access to that acute sense of horror and outrage that women often feel when they find themselves, or other women, being constituted through the male sexual gaze. The review was a sneering, prurient piece of writing that sniggered about Edward and Vivian preferring fellatio to kissing and professed amazement and disbelief about the 'new sex position' they had discovered in the bath. Reading the text of his review, re-viewing the film through the reviewer's eyes, I felt sickened and violated. I was so appalled at remembering just how it feels to be viewed in this way that I left the library without noting down the bibliographic details. As I walked back to my office I was both amazed at the fact that I had forgotten what it was like to be constituted in that way and totally vulnerable to the memory of it. In a similar vein, in talking to a close friend about the film, she told me she had been unable to watch it, since the talk she had heard before she saw it, filled with sexual innuendo, had made what she saw intolerable.

A male colleague, too, watched the video after I said how fascinated I was by it. His was an antagonistic viewing as well. He saw it as a trashy film about a rich guy who picks up a hooker (who is nothing, he said, like real hookers) for the weekend. And that was all there was to it, he said. He didn't notice that, despite the title, he had seen it as a film whose major protagonist was a man. In his viewing, Vivian was

103

not even a woman, but someone who belonged in that marginal (non-protagonist) category 'hooker'. Presumably one cannot, in such readings, be female, marginal and a protagonist. Feminist work that he had not had access to has done much to disrupt the marginalising and silencing of women and of particular categories of women, such as sex-workers. In novels such as Allende's *The House of Spirits* (Allende 1985), for example, the prostitute turns out to be, in some ways, the most powerful of all the characters.

Hite talks about Jean Rhys's characters' struggling to be read as both victim and protagonist without being judged and rejected. She points out that marginal characters (women and blacks, and, one might add, sex-workers) are usually flat characters without the complex tensions and motivations that drive the central (white male) protagonists. In contrast, she says:

> Rhys's protagonists are victims who are fully aware of their victimization. Their awareness does not make them any less victimized; it serves only to make them self-conscious in their roles and thus alienated from the society that wants to identify them completely with these roles. Worst of all, because their situation as both marginalized and wholly conscious is impossible in the terms proposed by the dominant culture, the statements in which they express their awareness cannot have any acknowledged context. If they do not speak 'in character', which is to say, in the wholly predictable ways that their role obliges, their utterances are received as senseless. To be outside the machine is to be without a language, condemned to emit sounds that inside interlocuters will interpret as evidence of duplicity, infantalism, hypocrisy—or simply madness.
>
> To women writers—indeed, to women generally in Western tradition—the imputation of madness is a continual and potent threat, for madness is the possibility that haunts their cultural identity as Other. Because the masculinist point of view is by definition the rational and intelligible one, anybody occupying the cultural position of 'woman' is at risk, required simultaneously to be a spokesman for this masculinist viewpoint and to embody its inverse or outside, the possibility of being *irr*ational, *un*intelligible. To express another point of view—to speak *as* 'woman' in this culture—is to utter truths by convention so unimaginable that they are likely to be dismissed as gibberish, mere symptoms of hysteria.

> (Hite 1989, p. 28)

My colleague's other comment on the film, offered as good reason to dismiss it, was its improbable ending. There is no way, he said, the rich guy is going to marry a hooker and ruin his career. Marginal characters, apparently, must stay marginal. He was angry with me for having talked about it as if it was worth watching, almost shouting at me in the photocopying room about what trash it was. Was it that it was trash, or was it that it broke the Western tradition in which:

> The hero must be male, regardless of the gender of the text-image, because the obstacle, what ever its personification, is morphologically female ... the hero, the mythical subject, is constructed as human being and as male; he is the active principle of culture, the establisher of distinction, the creator of differences. Female is what is not susceptible to transforma-

tion, to life or death; she (it) is an element of plot-space, a topos, a resistance, matrix and matter.

(de Lauretis 1984, pp. 118–19)

He was also disgusted that I should treat a popular text to such close scrutiny. I was treating it, he said, as if it were *King Lear*. By implication, I could hardly expect to be taken seriously as an academic if I could not distinguish 'Culture' from popular culture. Further, the film is clearly fantasy (Hollywood fantasy to boot) and therefore nothing to do with the real world. Of course, from a poststructuralist point of view, fantasy has everything to do with the real world, our fantasies and desires powerfully shaping the fictions that we call ourselves.

But all of this came after I had made an entirely different and positive reading. I had been invited to lecture to a class on men and film when in the USA. Being aware of the possibility of multiple readings of *Pretty Woman* I chose it as the basis of my lecture. I compared *Pretty Woman* to *The Paper Bag Princess* (Munsch & Marchenko 1980), which I had analysed in *Frogs and Snails and Feminist Tales* (Davies 1989b), showing that it is possible to read each text as one which confirms the status quo and one which disrupts it. The disruptive reading necessarily comes out of a context wherein that which is to be disrupted is present—so there is a representation of the status quo which is, in some manner, called into question. As Barthes says, when talking about redistributing or deconstructing language:

> . . . *such redistribution is always achieved by cutting.* Two edges are created: an obedient, conformist, plagiarizing edge (the language is to be copied in its canonical state, as it has been established by schooling, good usage, literature, culture), and *another edge*, mobile, blank (ready to assume any contours), which is never anything but the site of its effect: the place where the death of language is glimpsed. These two edges, *the compromise they bring about*, are necessary.

(Barthes 1989, p. 6)

In *The Paper Bag Princess* there is a traditional princess, Elizabeth, who is going to marry a prince named Ronald. The dragon steals the prince away and Elizabeth sets out to save him. She tricks the dragon into displaying all of his magical and masculine powers until he falls asleep and then she rushes into the dragon's cave to save Prince Ronald. But Prince Ronald rejects her as she no longer looks like a proper princess. Elizabeth tells Ronald that he looks like a proper prince but that he is a bum. And they don't get married after all.

This can be read as a feminist story in which the princess first gets caught up in the romantic storyline, then acts as the hero when this becomes necessary to save the prince. In being rejected by the prince for her heroic presence, she recognises that he is of no value to her and goes off alone. But it can also be read as a traditional romance that goes wrong, as many of the children in my preschool study did. The princess loses her princess status and won't listen to the prince when he tells her how to regain it by going and cleaning herself up and dressing again in princess clothes. Her foolish refusal means that she didn't deserve the prince and he will inevitably find someone else.

An even more conservative reading of this story became available to me when talking to people at Deakin University who were interested in masculinity, sport and representation. They noticed that Prince Ronald is not drawn as an hegemonic male. He is small and his posture is rather feminine. He plays tennis rather than the more masculine cricket or football. When the huge male dragon snatches him off, his little bum is pointed up in the air and clutched by the huge phallic claw of the dragon. Elizabeth's adventure with the male dragon, in this reading, is highly sexual. She is seductive at first, 'Is it true that you are the smartest and fiercest dragon in the whole world?' she asks. And when he performs his devastating and impressive feats she says such things as, 'Fantastic! Do it again!' until eventually the exhausted dragon falls into a deep sleep. Elizabeth rushes into the dragon's cave (a homosexual metaphor) and rejects Ronald (who did not after all seem at all eager to leave the cave) for being a 'bum'—again a metaphor for homosexual. In this reading, Prince Ronald's possible homosexuality is the reason he loses access to the princess and the romantic storyline. A profoundly heterosexist story emerges, absolutely confirming the status quo of heterosexual romance.

While children initially produce one reading or another, it is possible to work with such texts to enable them to see those multiple readings and to see how, by inserting themselves into the text and by focusing on and interpreting one rather than another set of textual details, they can create a text which repeats or disrupts familiar cultural patterns.

Similarly, with a popular text such as *Pretty Woman*. Here there are multiple layers of the traditional storyline: Cinderella, Pygmalion, Rapunzel, Little Red Riding Hood, Beauty and the Beast and the Prodigal Son all feature.

Cinderella

Vivian is a poor girl who is virtuous, and has been told she is bad. While on the one hand she accepts her lot, on the other, she longs for something better than the life she has. The fairy godmother (in this case Barney, the hotel manager, with some help from Edward) transforms her. She goes to the ball (the Opera) and the prince, Edward, falls in love with her. She flees leaving her glass slipper (the rubies) behind. Through these the prince finds her and they live happily ever after.

Pygmalion/My Fair Lady

Edward, the rich, powerful upper-class man transforms Vivian, the girl from the gutter (flower girl/prostitute). His interest in her at the outset is entirely professional and not personal. Many of the key moments hinge on class difference, the major question being is it possible for someone to transgress class boundaries by learning the style of the upper class if one has not been born into it. The scene at the polo (Ascot) is painful and humiliating because the act is flawed, her class background is revealed in a way she cannot control. Henry Higgins/Edward falls in love with her. The various versions of the ending of *Pygmalion/My Fair Lady* include Eliza striking out without Higgins to run a flower shop and falling in love and marrying. *Pretty Woman* has both these, first with Vivian, wearing androgynous clothes and going to San Francisco to complete her education, and then Vivian with long hair flowing, finding true love forever with Edward.

Rapunzel

Vivian, the beautiful princess in her tower, dreams of escape. The witch/queen (in this case, Stuckey the lawyer, representing traditional elite male values) holds her in her tower. She longs for escape. The prince, Edward, goes through a number of trials and tribulations (including dealing with his fear of heights) and climbs up the tower and rescues the princess.

Little Red Riding Hood

Vivian, the virtuous girl, strays from the path her mother has set for her. She is attracted to unworthy men (bums), and follows one of them (to LA) and finds she cannot go back. The wolf (men like Stuckey, the lawyer) preys on her. The father/woodchopper/good man (Barney the hotel manager and Edward) save her.

Beauty and the Beast

Edward is trapped inside a way of being that makes him appear negative and destructive. He needs Vivian's love to heal him. When, after much resistance, she finally kisses him and tells him she loves him it is transformative. Edward loses his beast-like qualities. Barthes says of the words 'I love you':

> What I want, deliriously, is to *obtain the word*. Magical, mythical? The Beast—held enchanted in his ugliness—loves Beauty; Beauty, obviously does not love the Beast, but at the end, vanquished (unimportant by what; let us say by the *conversations* she has with the Beast), she, too, says the magic word: 'Je vous aime, la Bete'; and immediately, through the sumptuous arpeggio of a harp, a new subject appears.
>
> (Barthes 1978 p. 153)

The Prodigal Son

Edward, the son, strays from the fold and does bad things (buying and breaking up companies) because he is angry with his father. He returns to the father (Morse), deciding to build things with him instead of breaking things up, and all is forgiven.

The disruptions that I saw in my early, 'innocent' viewings of the film were multiple. Some are made obvious and others are more subtle. The Cinderella story is openly disrupted in the conversation between Vivian and Kit after Vivian has fallen in love with Edward. Vivian says she has decided not to see him again. Kit first gets mad at Vivian for falling in love, despite all of her advice, but then suggests that it might work:

> Kit: Maybe you guys could like um you know get a house together and like buy some diamonds and a horse. I don't know. Anyway, it could work. It happens.

Vivian:	(laughs) When does it happen Kit? When does it really happen? Who does it really work out for? Does it work out with Skinny Marie or Rachel? No!
Kit:	Those are very specific cases of crack heads
Vivian:	I just want to know who it works out for. You give me one example of someone we know who it works out for
Kit:	Name someone. You want me to name someone. You want me to give you a name?
Vivian:	Yeah I want a name
Kit:	Oh my god, the pressure of a name (Kit presses her fingers to her temples while she tries to think of a name. She looks up smiling) Cinder-fuckin-rella! (They both laugh)

(Author's transcription)

And when Vivian leaves the hotel, walking away from Edward, and she says goodbye to Barney, he says:

Barney:	Well then I gather you are not accompanying Mr Lewis to New York?
Vivian:	Come on Barney you and me live in the real world, most of the time

The Rapunzel story is similarly shifted. Vivian's childhood dream was not of herself as virtuous and rewarded for her virtue, but resulted from being locked in the attic when she was bad. As a woman who has taken up a profession which transgresses all that woman should be, according to the hegemonic versions of womanhood, she nevertheless imagines that it is possible to insist that either she has the love and respect and commitment that are usually only accorded to virtuous women, or else she will walk off alone, like Princess Elizabeth, with her dignity and her self-respect intact. The 'saving' that is done in the film is reciprocal—not one-sided. Throughout the film, there is an influence of each on the other. Edward takes Vivian to the Opera and introduces her to culture. She introduces him to nature through simple pleasures, such as walking on grass with bare feet, reading together, wandering through the city streets. The nature/culture aspect of the male/female dualism is breached as each takes up as his/her own what the other has made available. Just as he makes elite culture available to her, she enables him to give up his male/elite control of emotions. He has paid a therapist ten thousand dollars to bring him to the point where he can say in a controlled way of his father, 'I am very angry with him'. In the rape scene, Edward is at first still tightly under control. When he says 'Bullshit' to Stuckey, it is in a quiet, tightly controlled voice. Eventually he finds the capacity to shout at Stuckey in full voice to 'Get out'. At the beginning, he does not notice people like Barney, sweeping them aside. At the end, he knows and calls him by his name and listens to him. Vivian persuades him to construct (albeit warships) rather than 'destruct' other people's companies. At the end of the film, when Edward climbs up the tower to rescue Vivian, she waits only for a moment and then climbs down the tower to meet him. He asks, when they embrace, 'So what happened after he climbed up the tower and rescued her?' and she answers, 'She rescues him right back'.

Neither Vivian nor Edward are flat characters who are either good or bad, powerful or powerless. Both are agents in control of their own fate and both are objects of the gaze. She is vulnerable and feminine, but she also is strong and has some traditional male characteristics—she drives brilliantly and knows all about cars; she often strides along in an angular, masculine way; she is active sexually in the sense of being able to take control of the sexual act, insisting on safety and being active in the face of Edward's passivity. She is able to talk about sex in humourous and clever ways. She utterly refuses the idea of having a pimp when Kit suggests it. She is in control—she says who, she says when, she says how much. She has the male version of her name. While it is possible to see the rape scene as a straightforward repetition of the traditional plot in which the sexually vulnerable woman is saved by the heroic male (who is made male and heroic through the agency of her vulnerability), it is also possible to see this as importantly different in that Vivian fights Stuckey strongly and has not been defeated by him when Edward turns up. In the end, Vivian walks away, despite Edward begging her to stay, and despite the fact that she wants to stay, because her reason tells her that the romantic dream cannot work out. For his part, Edward is powerful and rich but he also lacks many traditional male characteristics. He cannot express anger until the end of the film, he is emotional, he can't drive well, he gets lost, he is afraid of heights, he plays the piano.[3] On many occasions when Vivian is making a decision, such as to leave him, he does not order her to do otherwise as any traditional male would attempt to do. When they first get together, he is nervous about sex and prefers to talk first. Further, he is capable of being passive/receptive sexually—he lies back while Vivian seduces him. In an early shot of them sitting facing each other, she has her legs splayed apart in the traditional male assertive pose and he has his legs together.

The androgyny that is achieved for each of these characters is meshed with the class difference that they are struggling over. Many of Vivian's boyish characteristics could also be interpreted as working class, such as when she spits out her gum (and Edward says 'I don't believe you did that'). Similarly, Edward's incompetence with cars is attributed to his first car being a limousine. And Vivian can sit with her legs splayed because she is a hooker (and splayed legs in women are generally interpreted as sexual invitation (Wex 1985) but also because she is not a 'lady'.[4]

---

[3] And as Mc Clary (1991, p. 85) points out, 'Since Plato, music has been regarded as a very tricky medium that can corrupt, effeminize, bedazzle, and delude'. While Edward plays the piano, he also takes Vivian to the Opera. This may be read as an introduction to upper-class culture, but it can also be read as Edward introducing Vivian to the ultimate expression of feminine *jouissance*, a celebration of excess, of the abundant, feminine overflowing of emotion and passion, in both women and men, an expression probably unparalleled in any other art form in modern culture.

[4] This conflation between sexuality and class occurs in the talk of the primary-school children in *Shards of Glass* (Davies 1993) where it is discussed in some detail.

Very few, if any, of the students in the men and film class had seen these details that disrupt the traditional storylines. There were students in the class who expressed feminist outrage at the degrading exploitation of woman that they had seen the film to be about. The reading that we spent most time talking about was that provided by a young black man. He had been to see it with his male friends. What they had seen was a film in which the non-hero is trapped and destroyed by an evil woman.

M: The guys that I saw it with were—I mean when we first saw it we were like, well she virtually got everything out of the movie, because I mean, if we look at it just at face value, I mean she was a, she is still going to make it, then this guy comes, he pays her to stay with him for, how long, a week?

BD: A week. Yeah.

M: And, so she gets this money and then, at the end, they kind of get attached and she gets the guy and she has the money now and she is going to go off and live happily ever after. And then there was him, and he didn't—he gained her, but, but nobody knows that that's really going to work out, and so, I mean, what did he get out of all this?

BD: So, viewing it as a male, you didn't see the transformation, the prodigal son story, where he has gone away and become the destroyer and a user, and is drawn back, through his interaction with Vivian, to becoming a creator?

M: (Not really.)

BD: So he, he moves, in fact, from the, from (   ) the feminine side, the destructive chaotic side of the binary table, towards the male side, the creator, and becomes the one who builds things and makes things. That that just wasn't a powerful storyline for the males seeing it?

M: They—I mean a lot of the guys that I saw it with, I mean, like their dads own companies and stuff, and they like (we're not going to criticise what they do), because, I mean, here he was, a successful business man and all of a sudden he's going to stop doing what he was doing, that got him to the point of where he was, because he loved some girl

BD: So she destroyed him? *Huh!* ((laughter))

...

M: But if you think about society—society dictates that if you want to be successful in the business, you want to be successful in the business world you have to watch out for yourself. It's like to hell with everybody else, and if you lose that attitude it's kind of like losing your head, and all of a sudden here's this guy/

110

BD: So she robbed him of his masculinity?

M: (That is true)

BD: ((Laughter))

M: Well you said—I mean, you said 'losing your head', that means, you know, crudely you'd say 'losing your balls'

In this viewing, Edward is seen to be hopeless (not male, not a hero) from the outset of the film. He offends the masculinity of the viewers.

M: I was like 'what is this?' I mean, it was like this guy is driving—well the first thing that makes him look dumb, because he's got this expensive car that he can't drive and he's sitting there grinding the gears in this really expensive car, and—on the main street and he stops and this prostitute is going to get in and show him how to drive his car.

BD: So you were offended?

M: Yeah

BD: In masculine terms?

M: I mean—yeah. Yeah

And even earlier, he got upset when he broke off with his girlfriend, revealing that he is too emotional. As one of the young women in the class said, 'My brothers and my father didn't like Edward's character from the start because ( ) his girlfriend walked out and that and he got upset, and they said that a man wouldn't get that upset over his girlfriend.' Of such emotions Barthes comments:

Historically, the discourse of absence is carried on by the Woman: Woman is sedentary, Man hunts, journeys; Woman is faithful (she waits), man is fickle (he sails away, he cruises). It is Woman who gives shape to absence, elaborates its fiction, for she has time to do so; she weaves and she sings. . .It follows that in any man who utters the other's absence *something feminine* is declared ... A man is not feminised because he is inverted but because he is in love.

(Barthes 1978, pp. 13–14)

In this viewing, the emasculated Edward is trapped by an evil woman, the siren. Vivian is going to destroy him and take him for all he's got.

M: One of the things that is brought out when you watch this was that if they ever broke up—this was the setting of the movie ( ) if they ever broke up she didn't ( ) you know, trying to (drag out as much out of him as possible). That seems to be (a created

111

fear) and like, well at least where I went to school, (I) was always brought up with certain rules, especially this, that it's a—the kids in my school ( ) and they came from real powerful families and it's like they didn't—they didn't want to lose their power, its effect. They thought if women—they have seen it happen with other families (and they think that's how) ( ) but if you get divorced ( ) if you get divorced she is going to take everything you've got. They've always got that fear. I don't see it/

BD: I think—but you know, money equals power equals masculinity, and women, being the chaotic dangerous 'other', might take that power from you. Women are dangerous in this binary divide. They're the chaos. They will rob you of your masculinity if you're not careful, you can get sort of dragged into the feminine side, the chaotic side, instead of moving more power-fully towards goals/

M: And especially if those women happen to be women from another class. I mean it's bad enough if the woman in question is your own class, but if they've been socialised properly to know that that's not really what they ought to do—because maybe they have their own family money, right! I mean, but a woman like Vivian, right, a woman like Vivian is doubly dangerous.

BD: Yeah, Yeah

M: I think you've got—I don't think that's kind of right, because there are people that—the women that I think that I've heard them talk of, they—they've seen divorces where the women will take the money just to keep up their status quo with everybody else, you know, just to keep their/

M: Oh/

BD: That having married they've moved into the class of their husband/

M: And they want to stay there.

In this viewing, Stuckey rushes in quite rightly attempting to save Edward from his fate. He is outraged at the changes in Edward (taking a day off work, no longer breaking up companies but building things) and sees these as a result of Vivian's evil influence ('Stuckey's the one we relate to because that's what we see most of the time'). The man has become the plot-space being acted on by a woman who is a central protagonist, one who brings about changes. She can be only evil to have disrupted the normal order of things so badly. But in this reading, Stuckey tries to save the day by becoming the true (male) hero. He knows what to do with Vivian. He attempts to rape her. But foolish Edward, the non-hero, rushes in and stops the rape. He is his own worst enemy. He deserves what he gets—inevitable destruction.

112

This reading is similar to the Ronald-as-gay reading of *The Paper Bag Princess*. It underscores the traditional reading with gouging marks. Men struggle to be heroes, but they often fail. Because they are not real males they are vulnerable to women, to being destroyed and rejected by them. One must struggle to be the ascendant heterosexual male or face terrible consequences. One of the young women in the group said she had watched it with her father and that she had seen it that way, too, as a result of his reactions. In the group discussions, the young man who had offered this reading pondered on how significant it was that he had been with his mates when he saw the film. He could see the reading I had done as a potential reading and imagined that if he had seen it with his girlfriend and, therefore, partly viewed it through her eyes, he would have seen it as she might have seen it, that is as people overcoming their own limitations and learning to love each other:

M: She's more scared of—in the beginning of the movie she had that kind of stipulation that she wouldn't kiss a guy, and towards the end of the movie—they probably got more passionate with each other and everything, but it's like she lost that fear when she was with him. And it's (more or less)—some ( ) it kind of— (what am I trying to say here)—it kind of relates, like, to people having fears, like in relationships, and then it kind of breaks down over time. I guess what I'm trying to say is more or less when people get attached they see that ( ) like, it's like in the movie when people—like the people that I saw it with, they— how can I say it—they didn't really pick up on that part of it too much. I saw it with a bunch of guys and it's like—they didn't pick up on this too well ( ) like most of them are kind of macho, or you know, kind of (stuck) ( ) they think they aren't. They didn't pick up on it, and it's more or less like they could care less. They just thought it was, you know, just like ( ) and I thought that was kind of bad, (that some people think that).

These students thus struggled to catch themselves in the act of reading a story in their culture, to find themselves filling the silences and gaps, making meaning from context and available storylines, confirming the way they understood the world through fictions about that world, understanding this as a process on meaning-making, not a discovery of the 'real story' (though that was hard to let go of).[5]

McClary makes a similar point in her analysis of Madonna's video *Open Your Heart*. This video begins 'in the confined environment of a peep show. Madonna

---

[5] There are many ways in which this class could further research the storylines they were reading in *Pretty Woman*. One fruitful line of research would be to examine the myth of the siren destroying men who have not properly achieved their masculinity and to see in what ways the myth is tied to, or shifts with, changes, such as those brought about during the Enlightenment. How do changing social patterns impact on the male/female dualism? How do myths consolidate and make real those changes? How does this impact on, or intersect with, our own lived narratives? An interesting reading in addressing such questions would be Laqueur's *Making Sex: Body and Gender from the Greeks to Freud* (Laqueur 1990).

sings the song from the center of a carousel that revolves to display her to the gazes of customers peering safely from their cubicles.' In contrast, the music is extraordinary and exhilarating and 'the tension between the visual and musical dimensions of the video is extremely unsettling'. McClary's analysis is particularly interesting in light of the strong-woman-as-evil reading of *Pretty Woman*. She says:

> Like many of Madonna's strategies, the one she attempts in this video is quite audacious. For instance, the peep show situation is shot in such a way that the leering patrons are rendered pathetic and grotesque, while she alone lays claim to subjectivity: thus, the usual power relationship between the voyeuristic male gaze and object is here destabilized. Likewise, the young boy's game of impersonating the femme fatale and Madonna's transvestism at the end both refuse essentialist gender categories and turn sexual identity into a kind of play. Still, the video is risky, because for all those who have reduced her to a 'porn queen in heat', there she is: embodying that image to the max. Those features of the video that resist a reductive reading of this sort—the nonfit of the music, the power inversions, the narrative of escape to androgyny—can easily be overlooked. This is, of course, always the peril of attempting to deconstruct pornographic images: it becomes necessary to invoke the image in order to perform the deconstruction; but, once presented, the image is in fact there in all its glory.

(McClary 1991, p.162)

After the discussion with the men and film class, I decided to look at the film again—to try to catch myself in the act of viewing, to expose my own viewing to the same scrutiny that I had asked the students to undergo. Was I really sucked in by the romance but using a feminist rationalisation to make that seduction of myself acceptable? I decided, at the same time, to write about that viewing and re-viewing here, to use it as a vehicle for examining the relation between the self and fictional representations of self. I watched the film again several times, taking notes on what I saw, writing down the detail of actual dialogue and of moments in the film that seemed integral to my viewing of it. I realised that the opera scene was of *La Traviata,* an opera about a prostitute, with *Violetta* and *Alfredo* as the two lovers. Clearly it was no accident that *La Traviata* had been chosen and so I began to listen to *La Traviata* more closely as well.

So what, then, was the film that I began to see? I will try, in what follows, to catch myself in the act of constituting the text and myself in relation to it. By catching myself in the act of inserting myself in the text, of filling in the spaces, I can discover something of how I arrived at the original positive viewing.

Watching myself watching Vivian, then, I did not see the camera as looking at Vivian in an object-ionable way. It seemed to me it was with a loving eye that the camera picked out the detail of her being, including such details only someone who loves would notice, such as her scribbling black ink onto the scuffed bits of her boots before she put them on. When the camera first travels over her body at (what for me is) the beginning, I am puzzled as to why it might be someone else's body that was used for these shots, but am fairly rapidly drawn back into the portrayal of Vivian, escaping the rent collector by easefully climbing down the fire escape, walking with an easy stride through the city streets. One of the other prostitutes, Skinny Marie, has been killed. Vivian sees her being pulled out of a dumpster and is shocked and vulnerable. She is angry with Kit, her flat mate, for using their rent money for drugs and tells her so. But she and Kit have a good and loving relationship and the anger is resolved—they can, after all, earn the rent money. Friendships between women are affirmed as good and powerful.

Then along comes Edward in Stuckey's Lotus Esprit (the name suggesting fantasy/forgetfulness/life). He is driving incompetently. He asks Vivian for directions as he is lost. Again there are shots of her body that may not be hers, and again I am puzzled. The shots are, like the earlier ones, of a smooth, clean, utterly flawless, aesthetically pleasing body. An artwork of line and movement rather than a 'real' body. Vivian negotiates with Edward over paying her for directions and she takes him to his hotel. She very politely explains to him what he is doing wrong in his driving and he hands over the driving to her, which she does with power and competence, continuing her seduction of him at the same time. He is thus somewhat incompetent, though not bothered by that and also quiet and observant (a similar character to Alfredo in *La Traviata*). His powers of observation emerge in small comments such as his response to her claim that she earns $100 an hour, 'You make $100 an hour and you've got a safety pin holding your boot up? You've got to be joking!' When they arrive at the hotel, he does not want to pick her up and so she reluctantly turns to leave to go back to her 'office', as Edward calls it. But then he changes his mind and invites her into the hotel with gentlemanly manners, not treating her as dismissable and marginal: 'If you don't have any prior engagements I'd be pleased if you'd accompany me to the hotel.'

When they enter the lobby, she is overwhelmed by the opulence of the hotel yet, at the same time, refuses any objectifying gazes by making fools of those who presume to gaze in that way.

After Vivian and Edward have negotiated for her to stay for the week (a straight business deal) and she goes out to buy clothes, I am struck by the way she can be transformed into a member of the elite and yet not lose the person she was prior to that. The women in the shop who refuse to serve her, and the women at the polo appear to be lifeless mannikins, their elite manners and concerns having become all they are. Later, when Edward degrades her by telling Stuckey she is a hooker, she refuses to accept that degradation. She decides to leave. Edward further degrades her by throwing the money he owes her onto the bed instead of handing it to her. I am fascinated by the fact that there is a similar scene in *La Traviata* when Alfredo humiliates Violetta in front of others by throwing down at her feet the money he owes her, in a fit of jealousy. Vivian ignores the money and leaves. Edward follows her and asks her to stay on the grounds that he was jealous when he saw her talking to a young man at the polo. He does not force the issue, however. When the elevator arrives to take her down and the operator asks 'Down?', I expect Edward to say no, and am startled and impressed by his silence. He leaves the decision to Vivian and she chooses to stay.

The night at the opera is now the segment that holds most of my attention. When Edward hires the rubies for Vivian to wear to the Opera, he puts them on her and, again, he and the camera look at her lovingly. Again, unpredictably, he does not touch her. She is beautiful, and stands, for the moment, seeing her own image in the

115

mirror, separate in her own space. At the opera they sit in the proscenium box, Vivian the (now) high-class hooker, about to watch an opera about a high-class hooker.

In reading about *La Traviata* in the booklet accompanying the CD, I found the following description of Marie Duplessis. Marie was a well known and beautiful courtesan who lived in Paris and on whom the original heroine in *La Traviata* was based. Someone who knew Marie wrote at the time:

> In all the splendour of a benefit performance at the Opéra, we suddenly saw one of the great proscenium boxes opened, with a certain noise, and that beauty advanced, a bouquet in her hand [...] She was ravishingly coiffed, her beautiful hair entwined with diamonds and flowers and pinned up with that studied grace that gave movement and life; her arms and bosom were bare, and she wore necklaces, bracelets, emeralds.

(Janin, cited in Weaver 1981, p. 10)

So in the scene at the Opera, not only do we now have Vivian watching Violetta, but we have Vivian sitting where Marie Duplessis sat, in the proscenium box, looking like Marie (though with rubies rather than emeralds), and being looked at (by me) with appreciation, in the way Marie was looked at by Janin. And she is looking at the woman whose story was based on Marie's story. This is a poststructuralist's dream! Layer upon layer of life and fiction until it simply is not possible to tell which is which.

The particular excerpts from the Opera are fascinating. First we see Violetta singing with a woman (Kit and Vivian). Then we see her singing to Alfredo of her love for him and his longing for her to love him. She does this at the very point where she is, unbeknown to him, leaving him. She has been persuaded by Alfredo's father that she must give him up because her past as courtesan will ruin him. She sings:

> Amami, Alfredo,
>
> Amami quant'io t'amo!
>
> Addio!
>
> (Love me, Alfredo,
>
> Love me, as I love you!
>
> Farewell!)

We see Vivian deeply immersed in and moved by this scene. This is followed immediately by the death scene. In the opera, Alfredo has just returned, having realised the sacrifice Violetta made for him and how much he loves her, but too late. As she dies, she sings:

> [In me rinasce,]
>
> M'agita insolito vigor!

116

Ah! ma io ritorno a viver!

O gioia!

(I feel reborn in me the strength

That once was mine!

I feel I'm coming back to life!

Oh joy!)

The camera lovingly focuses on Vivian's immersion in this moment. Edward looks lovingly at Vivian looking at the opera. I look at him loving her and then at her overwhelmed by Violetta's death and I am crying, too, as I watch Vivian crying. Only at his moment of total loss does Alfredo know his love for Violetta, and at the same moment Edward recognises his love for Vivian.

The last few lines of the (actual) opera are missed out:

Oh, heavens! She is dying!

Violetta?

Oh God, she needs help!

She is dead!

Oh my grief!

We are left then with Violetta's life affirming words and Vivian's grief. I think about McClary talking about Clément talking about opera:

In the final pages of *Opera*, Clément delivers an invocation for all the women victims of the operatic stage. For she loves them, has felt their magnificent, subversive voices to be inspiring and powerful—despite the law that has demanded their deaths. What she hopes for the future is the emergence of women who (like Carmen) can enjoy their erotic energy and still say no when they please but who, (unlike Carmen) are permitted to survive—women who form a sisterhood that can sing freely and who cannot, *will not*, be driven underground.

(McClary 1988, p. xvii)

Can Vivian be read as precisely that?

What is happening here with the binaries of life and death, of male and female? A common motif in our traditional literate history is the bringing of these two binaries together, creating the possibility of (man) transcending them. Here Vivian and Edward are both and neither, thus transcending male/female and life/death.

In achieving this viewing of *Pretty Woman*, I constitute it as a text in which the

117

first two deconstructive steps are taken in reversing these binaries—privileging life, woman's life, over her death.

The night after the opera, Edward and Vivian make love in a way that reminds me of Irigaray's two hands touching in prayer—each hand both subject and object—neither in control of the other—touching as two lips touch. (Two lips like women's labia, symbolising woman's wholeness; two lips that kiss for the first time, the intimacy of that first kiss signalling the shift from the business deal they had, to intimate love and respect for each other). The visual aspects of this scene are of perfect symmetry. Two sets of arms entwine the other with absolute harmony of line and reciprocity of encirclement.

Next morning they are confronted with the fact of their last night together. He suggests that he put her up in an apartment so they can see each other again. She says no. Once it would have been enough, but he has changed all that and now that is not enough. She says:

> When I was a little girl, my mumma used to lock me in the attic when I was bad, which was pretty often. And I would, I would pretend I was a princess trapped in a tower by a wicked queen. And then suddenly this knight, on a white horse with his colours flying would come charging up and draw his sword, and I would wave, and he would climb up the tower and rescue me. But never in all the time that I had this dream, did the knight say to me 'come on baby I'll put you up in a great condo'.

> (Author's transcription)

Edward says he has heard what she has said, but doesn't know what to do. He says he has never treated her like a hooker—which is true until this moment, except perhaps for the angry moment when he throws her money down on the bed. But now he has. Vivian refuses this transformation back into marginal status and decides to leave. He asks her to stay but she says she can't. Edward experiences great pain when she leaves, but seems resigned to losing her. It is at this point that Barney intervenes again. Earlier he has commented to Edward that she is interesting. Now he comments enigmatically, apparently referring to the rubies, that it must be hard to let go of something so beautiful. He gives Edward the information he needs to find Vivian and to play out her childhood fantasy in which the bad girl is nonetheless rewarded.

The last sequence of the film takes on a dream-like quality. When Edward drives up to her apartment in the white limousine, waving his umbrella (sword), the music in the background is that double moment at which Violetta declares her love, knowing that she and Alfredo are about to part:

> Amami, Alfredo,

> Amami quant'io t'amo!

> Addio!

As Edward and Vivian embrace, Violetta sings 'Addio!' Just as Violetta affirms love as she leaves Alfredo, and dies affirming life at the same time, so Edward and

Vivian join as the words tell the opposite. This is followed immediately by the words from the song *Pretty Woman*, 'Are you lonely just like me, pretty woman?'[6]

In my reading of the ending, the contradictions are no longer contradictions but a collapsing of binary opposites into a moment of transcendence. I experience a moment of bliss. Not pleasure at a predictable ending, I am usually completely impatient with stories that give the boring old romantic ending—such as happens in the film *Wings of Desire* (Dir. Wim Wenders), for example—but bliss at the disruption to the hegemonic version of the male/female dualism which, at the same time, allows me to appreciate that woman can be all, can transgress, can be loved. It is a film that gives me permission to be strong and assertive, to decide to go it alone at the same time as it gives permission to be feminine and opens up the (impossible) possibility of being loved while being all of these.[7]

The final scene shifts back to Hollywood and the same young black man striding through the streets of Hollywood, whom we glimpsed at the beginning, saying:

> Welcome to Hollywood. What's your dream? Everybody comes here. This is Hollywood. Some dreams come true, some don't, but keep on dreaming.

The words bring me back to the fact that this is a fantasy, moreover a Hollywood fantasy.

I suspect for those for whom the film is merely pleasure, or even a source of anger, that it moves too gently. For such viewers the experience of disruption/bliss may require more angry and disruptive re-tellings of the traditional stories, so we know without doubt that we are being unsettled from our familiar patterns. Dorothy Hewett's *Grave Fairytale* (Hewett 1991) is one such disruptive telling:

---

[6] According to the reviews, the original script was much darker, pointing up the parallels between corporate raiding and prostitution. In the original script, both Edward and Vivian come to a bad end, she committing suicide and he being accused of her murder. While this ending is rejected both by the director and any people I have talked to about it, most people also feel unhappy about the marriage-happy-ever-after ending as well, since it does not ring true and it appears to seduce us back into the utterly conservative pre-feminist dream of the heterosexual couple and the nuclear family. Feminism is colonised by the American dream. An interesting task for those who want new storylines would be to write another ending—or perhaps this is one of those stories that at this particular point in time needs multiple endings. As in the film *Thelma and Louise,* where the ending is completely enigmatic (did they kill themselves or did they take on super human proportions and escape by flying), the ending of *Pretty Woman* seems to me also, quite enigmatic, holding the possibility of multiple readings.

[7] Barthes does not define *bliss*, that which disrupts, as something one could enjoy—it is more an improbable mixture of extreme pleasure and extreme pain. *Pleasure*, in contrast, can be euphoric, but is also stultifying. I doubt whether it is possible to say of any experience of text that this is 'bliss', not 'pleasure', or 'pleasure', not 'bliss'. If disruptions to the familiar make possible a world one longs to move towards, the bliss may well not be experienced as pain, but rather as a welcome break from the stultifying effects of the familiar.

119

Grave Fairytale

I sat in my tower, the seasons whirled,
the sky changed, the river grew
and dwindled to a pool.
The black Witch, light as an eel,
laddered up my hair
to straddle the window-sill.

She was there when I woke, blocking the light,
or in the night, humming, trying on my clothes.
I grew accustomed to her; she was as much a part of me
as my own self; sometimes I thought, 'She *is* myself!'
a posturing blackness, savage as a cuckoo.

There was no mirror in the tower.

Each time the voice screamed from the thorny garden
I'd rise and pensively undo the coil,
I felt it switch the ground, the earth tugged at it,
once it returned to me knotted with dead warm birds
once wrapped itself three times around the tower—the tower quaked.
Framed in the window, whirling the countryside
 with my great net of hair I'd catch a hawk, a bird, and once a bear.
One night I woke, the horse pawed at the walls,
the cell was full of light, all my stone house
suffused, the voice called from the calm white garden, 'Rapunzel'.
I leant across the sill, my plait hissed out and spun like hail;
he climbed, slow as a heartbeat, up the stony side,
we dropped together as he loosed my hair,
his foraging hands tore me from neck to heels:
the witch jumped up my back and beat me to the wall.

Crouched in a corner I perceived it all,
the thighs jack-knifed apart, the dangling sword thrust home,
pinned like a specimen—to scream with joy.

I watched all night the beasts unsatisfied
roll in their sweat, their guttural cries
made the night thick with sound.
Their shadows gambolled, hunch-backed, hairy-arsed,
and as she ran four-pawed across the light,
the female dropped coined blood spots on the floor.

When morning came he put his armour on,
kissing farewell like angels swung on hair.
I heard the metal shoes trample the round earth about my tower.
Three times I lent my hair to the glowing prince,
hand over hand he climbed, my roots ached,
the blood dribbled on the stone sill.
Each time I saw the frame-faced bully boy sick with his triumph.

The third time I hid the shears,
a stab of black ice dripping in my dress.
He rose, his armour glistened in my tears,
the convex scissors snapped,
the glittering coil hissed, and slipped through air to undergrowth.
His mouth, like a round O, gaped at his end,
his finger nails ripped out, he clawed through space.
His horse ran off flank-deep in blown thistles.
Three seasons he stank at the tower's base.
A hawk plucked out his eyes, the ants busied his brain,
the mud-weed filled his mouth, his great sword rotted,
his tattered flesh-flags hung on bushes for the birds.

Bald as a collaborator I sit walled in the thumb-nosed tower,
wound round three times with autumn leaves.
And the witch ... sometimes I idly kick
a little heap of rags across the floor.
I notice it grows smaller every year.

(Hewett 1991, pp. 50–1)

Here the good/bad binarism is collapsed and gone beyond. Death becomes the prince's death and the woman is left in her 'thumb-nosed tower' with the light-blocking witch in her, dwindling every year. Her anger at the absurdity of the traditional romance and the part men play in it is powerfully told.

Pretty Woman does not so obviously confront and dismantle woman-as-object, and so there is always the dangerous possibility that Vivan will be read in pornographic ways. On the other hand, she is capable of drawing us towards her in a way Hewett's character might not be.

What have I done then with my various tellings of my own and others' readings of *Pretty Woman*? I have tried to make visible the routes by which we each got there, not as a set of guideposts to a possible true telling, but, like the collective biography strategies, as a way of seeing how one might catch oneself in the act of being constituted and, at the same time, coming to see how it is that we, as readers and viewers, constitute texts and lives. In coming to see the power of context to dictate the discourses we draw on, we can see both self and world shifting with those discourses as they change and intersect. And in coming to see the multiple possible readings of any text, and to see the ways in which our own readings are constituted out of the discursive possibilities known to us, we can open up the possibility of different discursive practices and new fictional and lived storylines.

What is important here is not the issue of whether there are many texts or one text, whether there are multiple readings or there should be one true, authoritative reading, but the process of coming to understand one's embeddedness in discourse, the interaction between oneself and text, and the vulnerability we have to 'authoritative' versions of text. The challenge is to find ways of catching ourselves in the act of constituting and being constituted and to find ways to attend to the power of discursive practices as we use them to make lives and worlds.

Strategies such as the one I have used here with *Pretty Woman* disrupt the unquestioned authority of author and text, and of teacher as arbiter of textual meanings. In achieving not only multiple readings but in looking at how they are achieved, we find another way of disrupting the individual/social binary. And in loosening the grip of authority, we open up the possibility of our own authorship, our own storylines, both as they trap us in old patterns and as they might liberate us. We learn to see the stultifying grip of repeated cultural patterns and open up the blissful possibility of new patterns, which break apart old binaries and open up the possibility of multiplicity.

A concluding comment

Equity strategies have generally been of an add-on kind, leaving the bulk of old discursive practices in place. The implication of poststructuralist theory is the need for a re-visioning of discursive practices and a re-writing of curriculum and of school texts that make the source of their claims to authority visible. Such visibility would invite both students and teachers to interrogate the texts and to see the constitutive force of the language and the images through which 'real worlds' are constituted, as well as the power of all that is left unsaid. If teachers and curriculum designers and authors of educational texts are to take the poststructuralist turn, we need to begin with ourselves and our own lives, to find strategies to locate the ways in which we are caught up in the multiple discursive practices that shape our everyday worlds, to find how authority is constituted and with what effect.

I have suggested here some strategies for beginning to work differently in writing and interpreting texts, and for the readings we do in, and of, our own lives and the lives of others. There are many more ways you, too, might invent to disrupt the male/ female dualism, to undo the plagiarising repetition of old patterns, and to make possible a new relation with language through which the unimaginable can begin to be imagined, and through which the stories of our lives can begin to be lived differently.

References

ABC TV (1992), *Whitlam.*

Allende, I. (1985), *The House of Spirits,* Black Swan, London.

Atkinson, P. & Delamont, S. (1976), 'Mock-ups and cock-ups:The stage management of guided discovery instruction', in M. Hammersley & P. Woods (eds), *The Process of Schooling: A Sociological Reader,* Routledge & Kegan Paul in association with The Open University Press, London.

Atwood, M. (1992), 'The bog man', *Wilderness Tips,* Virago, London.

Baker, C.D. (1991), 'Reading the texts of reading lessons', *Australian Journal of Reading,* vol. 14 , no. 1.

Baker, C.D. & Davies, B. (1989), 'A lesson in sex roles', *Gender and Education,* vol. 1, no. 1, pp. 59–76.

Barthes, R. (1978), *A Lover's Discourse: Fragments,* Penguin, Harmondsworth, UK.

Barthes, R. (1989), *The Pleasure of the Text,* (trans.) Richard Miller, The Noonday Press, New York.

Brodribb, S. (1992), *Nothing Mat(t)ers: A Feminist Critique of Postmodernism,* Spinifex Press, Melbourne.

Castor, L. (1991), 'Did she or didn't she?: The discourse of scandal in the 1988 US presidential campaign', *Genders,* vol. 12, pp. 62–76.

Chappell, A. (1984), 'Family fortunes: a practical photography project', in A. McRobbie & M. Nava (eds), *Gender and Generation,* Macmillan, London, pp. 112–29.

Clark, M. (1989), *The Great Divide: The Construction of Gender in the Primary School,* Curriculum Development Centre, Canberra.

Cole, B. (1986), *Princess Smartypants,* Hamish Hamilton, London.

Connell, R.W. (1987), *Gender and Power,* Allen & Unwin, Sydney.

Curthoys, A. (1991), 'The three body problem', *Hecate,* vol. 17, no. 1, pp. 14–21.

Conley, V. A (1991), *Hélène Cixous: Writing the Feminine,* expanded edn, University of Nebraska Press, Lincoln, Nebr. & London.

Davies, B. (1989a), 'Education for sexism: A theoretical analysis of the sex/gender bias in education', *Educational Philosophy and Theory,* vol. 21, no. 1, pp. 1–19.

Davies, B (1989b), *Frogs and Snails and Feminist Tales: Preschool Children and Gender,* Allen & Unwin, Sydney.

Davies, B. (1990a), 'The problem of desire', *Social Problems,* vol. 37, no. 4, pp. 801–16.

Davies, B. (1990b), 'Agency as a form of discursive practice: A classroom scene observed', *British Journal of Sociology of Education*, vol. 11, no. 3, pp. 341–61.

Davies, B. (1991), 'The concept of agency: A feminist poststructuralist analysis', *Social Analysis*, special issue on 'Postmodern critical theorising', vol. 30, pp. 42–53.

Davies, B. (1992), 'Women's subjectivity and feminist stories', in C. Ellis & M. Flaherty (eds), *Investigating Subjectivity: Research on Lived Experience*, Sage, Newbury Park, Calif.

Davies, B. (1993), *Shards of Glass: Children Reading and Writing Beyond Gendered Identities*, Allen & Unwin, Sydney.

Davies, B. & Harré, R. (1990), 'Positioning: The discursive production of selves', *Journal for the Theory of Social Behaviour*, vol. 20, pp. 43–63.

Davies, B. & Munro, K. (1987), 'The perception of order in apparent disorder: A classroom scene observed', *Journal of Education for Teaching*, vol. 13, pp. 117–31.

de Lauretis T. (1984), *Alice Doesn't: Feminism, Semiotics, Cinema*, Indiana University Press, Bloomington, Illin.

de Lauretis T. (ed.) (1986), *Feminist Studies/ Critical Studies*, Indiana University Press, Bloomington, Illin.

Derrida, J. (1991a), 'Of *Grammatology*', in P. Kamuf (ed.), *A Derrida Reader: Between the Blinds*, Harvester Wheatsheaf, New York.

Derrida, J. (1991b), 'Tympan', in Kamuf, P. (ed.), *A Derrida Reader: Between the Blinds*, Harvester Wheatsheaf, New York.

Derrida, J. (1991c), 'The Double Session', in Kamuf, P. (ed.), *A Derrida Reader: Between the Blinds*, Harvester Wheatsheaf, New York.

Diamond, I. & Quinby, L. (1988), *Feminism and Foucault: Reflections on Resistance*, Northeastern University Press, Boston.

Durrell, L. (1962), *The Alexandria Quartet*, Faber & Faber, London.

Eribon, D. (1991), *Michel Foucault*, Faber & Faber, London.

Foucault, M. (1972), *The Archaeology of Knowledge*, Tavistock, London.

Foucault, M. (1977), 'What is an author?', in D. Bouchard (ed.), *Language, Counter-memory, Practice*, Cornell University Press, Ithaca, NY.

Foucault, M. (1980), *The History of Sexuality*, vol .1, Vintage, New York.

Fraser, N. (1992), 'The uses and abuses of French discourse theories for feminist politics', in N. Fraser & S. L. Bartky, *Revaluing French Feminism: Critical Essays on Difference, Agency and Culture*, Indiana University Press, Bloomington, Illin.

Gilbert, P. & Taylor, S. (1991), *Fashioning the Feminine*, Allen & Unwin, Sydney.

Gordon , L. (1986), 'What's new in women's history', in de Lauretis T. (ed.), *Feminist Studies/ Critical Studies*, Indiana University Press, Bloomington, Illin.

Gore, J. M. (1992), *The Struggle for Pedagogies: Critical and Feminist Discourses as Regimes of Truth*, Routledge, New York.

Grosz, E. (1989), *Sexual Subversions: Three French Feminists*, Allen & Unwin, Sydney.

Grosz, E. (1990), 'Inscriptions and body-maps: Representations and the body corporeal', in T. Threadgold & A. Cranny-Francis (eds), *Feminine, Masculine and Representation*, Allen & Unwin, Sydney.

Grosz, E. (1992), Refiguring lesbian desire, unpublished paper, Monash University, Melbourne.

Hanmer, J. (1990), 'Men, power and the exploitation of women', in J. Hearn & D. Morgan (eds), *Men, Masculinities and Social Theory*, Unwin Hyman, London.

Haug, F. *et al.* (1987), *Female Sexualisation*, Verso, London.

Hewett, D. (1991), *Grave Fairytale*, in *Dorothy Hewett: Selected Poems*, Fremantle Arts Centre Press, South Fremantle, WA.

Hite, M. (1989), *The Other Side of the Story: Structure and Strategies of Contemporary Feminist Narratives*, Cornell University Press, Ithaca.

Kimmel, M. (1990), 'After fifteen years: The impact of the sociology of masculinity on the masculinity of sociology', in J . Heam & D. Morgan, (eds), *Men, Masculinities and Social Theory*, Unwin Hyman, London.

Kingston, M.H. (1977), *The Woman Warrior: Memoirs of a Girlhood Among Ghosts*, Random House, New York.

Kress, G. (1985), *Linguistic Processes in Sociocultural Practice*, Deakin University Press, Geelong, Vic.

Kristeva, J. (1981), 'Women's time', (trans.) A. Jardine, *Signs*, vol. 7, no. 1.

Lakoff, G. & Johnson, M. (1980), *The Metaphors We Live By*, University of Chicago Press, Chicago.

Laqueur, T. (1990), *Making Sex: Body and Gender from the Greeks to Freud*, Harvard University Press, Cambridge

Lather, P. (1991), *Getting Smart: Feminist Research and Pedagogy with/in the Postmodern*, Routledge, New York.

Little, G. (1986), 'Whitlam, Whitlamism and the Whitlam years', in *The Whitlam Phenomenon*, McPhee Gribble/Penguin, Ringwood, Vic.

McClary, S. (1988), Foreword to C. Clément, *Opera, or the Undoing of Women*, University of Minnesota Press, Minn.

McClary, S. (1991), *Feminine Endings: Music, Gender, and Sexuality*, University of Minnesota Press, Minn.

McDermott, R. P. (1976), Kids make sense: An ethnographic account of the interactional management of success and failure in one first grade classroom, unpublished PhD thesis, Stanford University, Calif.

Macintyre, S. (1992), 'Rethinking Australian citizenship', Cunningham Lecture, *Academy of Social Sciences in Australia*, Canberra.

Martin, B. (1988), 'Feminism, criticism and Foucault', in I. Diamond & L. Quinby, *Feminism and Foucault. Reflections on Resistance*, Northeastern University Press, Boston.

Modjeska, D. (1990), *Poppy*, McPhee Gribble/Penguin, Ringwood, Vic.

Moi, T. (1985), *Sexual/Textual Politics*, Methuen, London.

Munsch, R. & Marchenko, M. (1980), *The Paper Bag Princess*, Annik Press, Toronto.

Ong, W. (1982), *Orality and Literacy: The Technologizing of the Word*, Methuen, London.

Orr, J. (1990) , 'Theory on the market: Panic incorporating', *Social Problems*, vol. 37, no. 4, pp. 460–84.

Reid, E., (1986), 'Creating a policy for women', in *The Whitlam Phenomenon*, McPhee Gribble/Penguin, Ringwood, Vic., pp. 145–55.

Sarup, M. (1988), *An Introductory Guide to Post-structuralism and Postmodernism*, Harvester Wheatsheaf, New York.

Tannen, D. (1990), *You Just Don't Understand: Women and Men in Conversation*, William Morrow & Co., New York.

Walkerdine, V. (1989), 'Femininity as performance', *Oxford Review of Education*, vol. 15, pp. 267–79.

Walkerdine, V. (1993), 'Sex, power and pedagogy', in M. Alvarado, E. Buscombe & R. Collins (eds), *The Screen Education Reader*, Macmillan, London.

Walkerdine, V. & Lucey, H. (1989), *Democracy in the Kitchen: Regulating Mothers and Socialising Daughters*, Virago, London.

Weaver, W. 'Alphonsine, Marie, Marguerite, Violetta, and Guiseppe Verdi', in the booklet accompanying the recording of *La Traviata*, Decca.

Weedon, C. (1987), *Feminist Practice and Poststructuralist Theory*, Oxford, Blackwell.

Wex, M. (1979), *Let's Take Back our Space: Female and Male Body Language as a Result of Patriarchal Structures*, Frauenliteraturverlag Hermine Fees, Berlin.

Wilshire, D. (1989), 'The uses of myth, image, and the female body in re-visioning knowledge', in A. M. Jagger & S. R. Borno (eds), *Gender/body/ knowledge: Feminist Reconstructions of Being and Knowing*, Rutgers University Press, New Brunswick, pp. 92–114.

Wittig, M. (1980), 'The straight mind', *Feminist Issues*, vol. 1.